Contents

Module 19	1
Module 20	13
Module 21	23
Module 22	34
Module 23	46
Module 24	58
Module 25	69
Module 26	81
Module 27	93
Module 28	103
Module 29	116
Module 30	127
Module 31	139
Module 32	151
Module 33	162
Module 34	173
Module 35	185
Module 36	196

© 2020 by Accelerate Education
Visit us on the Web at: www.accelerate.education

Writing First Draft

Name _____

Topic: Growing Up

Think about a time when you went through something important or learned a lesson. How did that make you grow up a little more?

Details:

Name: _____

Spelling - Growing Up

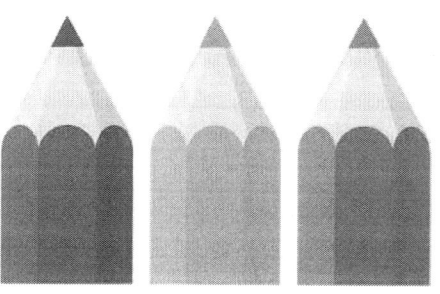

Rainbow Words

Directions:
Please choose three different colored pencils. Write each spelling word three times using each color.

under

over

never

water

center

border

fever

number

whether

tower

labor

flavor

author

horror

continued on the next page...

19.2 - Growing Up

Spelling - Growing Up

Rainbow Words

Directions:
Please choose three different colored pencils. Write each spelling word three times using each color.

sailor _____ _____ _____

anchor _____ _____ _____

odor   _____ _____ _____

error   _____ _____ _____

color   _____ _____ _____

motor   _____ _____ _____

Name: _____

DIRECTIONS:
Use this graphic organizer to start brainstorming ideas for your story.

GROWING UP
Story Graphic Organizer

How will you introduce your character? What are his/her characteristics? What do we need to know about him or her?

Introduction of Character:

What is the problem in your story? What is the character facing?

Problem:

What is the solution to the problem?
How does the character grow up because of this problem?

Solution:

19.2 - Growing Up

GROWING UP
Handwriting Practice

Name _____

Directions:
Use the dashed lines to help you connect the letters together.

Example:

GROWING UP
Vocabulary Crossword Puzzle

Name: _____

DIRECTIONS:
Use the definitions to complete the crossword puzzle using your vocabulary words.

ACROSS:
3 a young bird not yet able to leave the nest

4 to push roughly

6 to follow as a pattern, model, or example

DOWN:
1 to win over to a belief or action by argument or serious request

2 a violently unfriendly or aggressive attitude

5 rarely

19.3 - Growing Up

Name: _____

GROWING UP
Spelling Worksheet

Directions:
Fill in the blanks with an *er* or *or* to correctly spell each word.

1. lab____ ____
2. ov ____ ____
3. auth____ ____
4. od ____ ____
5. anch ____ ____
6. wat ____ ____
7. err ____ ____
8. wheth ____ ____
9. bord ____ ____
10. col ____ ____

11. horr ____ ____
12. flav ____ ____
13. nev ____ ____
14. numb ____ ____
15. und ____ ____
16. sail ____ ____
17. fev ____ ____
18. tow ____ ____
19. mot ____ ____
20. cent ____ ____

7

19.4 - Growing Up

Name: _____

GROWING UP
Story Checklist

Directions:
Reread your writing carefully. Put a ✓ check in each box under Author Check as you complete each item.

Author check: **Revise and Edit for the following:**

1. **Clarity and Meaning:** Ask yourself:
   - ☐ "Does the story introduce and describe the main character?"
   - ☐ "Is the problem in the story clear?"
   - ☐ "Is the solution in the story clear?"
   - ☐ "Did the character in the story learn a lesson or grow up?"
   - ☐ Rewrite parts that need revision.

2. **Correct Use of Words:** Ask yourself:
   - ☐ "Are specific adjectives used to describe the person?"
   - ☐ "Are the problem and solution explained well?"
   - ☐ "Do the sentences sound good together?"
   - ☐ Rewrite parts that need revision.

3. **Capitalization:**
   - ☐ Use capitals at the beginning of each sentence and for every name.
   - ☐ Make corrections if needed.

4. **Punctuation:**
   - ☐ Use periods, exclamation points, and question marks.
   - ☐ Did you use dialogue? Make sure it is punctuated correctly.
   - ☐ Make corrections if needed.

5. **Spelling:**
   - ☐ Check for correct spelling.
   - ☐ Make corrections if needed.

Name: _____

GROWING UP
Handwriting Practice 2

Directions:
Connect the letters across each line like the example below.

Example:

ccccccccccccccccccccccccccccccccccc

GROWING UP

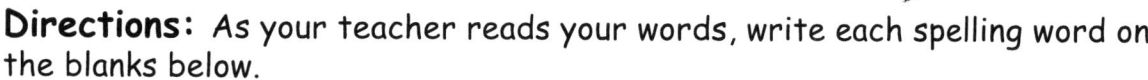

Name _____

SPELLING TEST

Directions: As your teacher reads your words, write each spelling word on the blanks below.

1) _____
2) _____
3) _____
4) _____
5) _____
6) _____
7) _____
8) _____
9) _____
10) _____
11) _____
12) _____

13) _____
14) _____
15) _____
16) _____
17) _____
18) _____
19) _____
20) _____

Name: _____

GROWING UP
Jolly Robin Character Description

Directions:
Please complete each section below after reading "Jolly Robin."

What is the character's problem?	How is the problem solved?

Character's Name: _____
Illustration:

How would you describe the character?	How did the character change over time?

11

19.5 - Growing Up

GROWING UP

Name _____

Independent Reading

Directions: Read your independent reading book for 30 minutes. When you are done, describe the main character of the story.

I read _____ by _____
          (book title)   (author)

for 30 minutes today.

_____   _____
My Signature   Parent/Guardian Signature

Details

Describe the main character in the story that you read today.

_____
_____
_____
_____
_____
_____
_____

Name _____

Journal Entry

Directions: Write your response to the prompt on the lines below. Don't forget to check for complete sentences as you write.

Prompt: Think of a time when you did something nice for someone or someone did something nice for you. Write about it below.

_____
_____
_____
_____
_____
_____
_____
_____
_____
_____
_____
_____
_____
_____
_____
_____

20.1 - Good Deeds

Name: _____

Spelling - Good Deeds

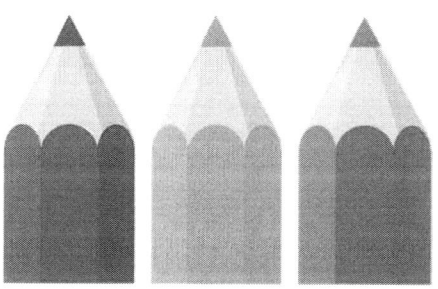

Rainbow Words

Directions:
Please choose three different colored pencils. Write each spelling word three times using each color.

wonder _____ _____ _____

mother _____ _____ _____

father _____ _____ _____

weather _____ _____ _____

washer _____ _____ _____

silver _____ _____ _____

water _____ _____ _____

shower _____ _____ _____

leader _____ _____ _____

tractor _____ _____ _____

junior _____ _____ _____

factor _____ _____ _____

favor _____ _____ _____

rumor _____ _____ _____

continued on the next page...

20.2 - Good Deeds

Spelling - Good Deeds

Rainbow Words

Directions:
Please choose three different colored pencils. Write each spelling word three times using each color.

minor _____ _____ _____

actor _____ _____ _____

tutor _____ _____ _____

visor _____ _____ _____

Name: _____

Handwriting
Practice 1

Directions:
Use the dashed lines to help you connect the letters together.

Example:

cdcdcdcdcdcdcdcdcdcdcdcdcdc

gogogogogogogogogogogogo

cgcgcgcgcgcgcgcgcgcgcg

dodododododododododododo

cocococococococococococ

dgdgdgdgdgdgdgdgdgdgdgd

20.2 - Good Deeds

Name: _____

Good Deeds
Vocabulary Crossword Puzzle

Directions: Use the definitions to complete the crossword puzzle using your vocabulary words.

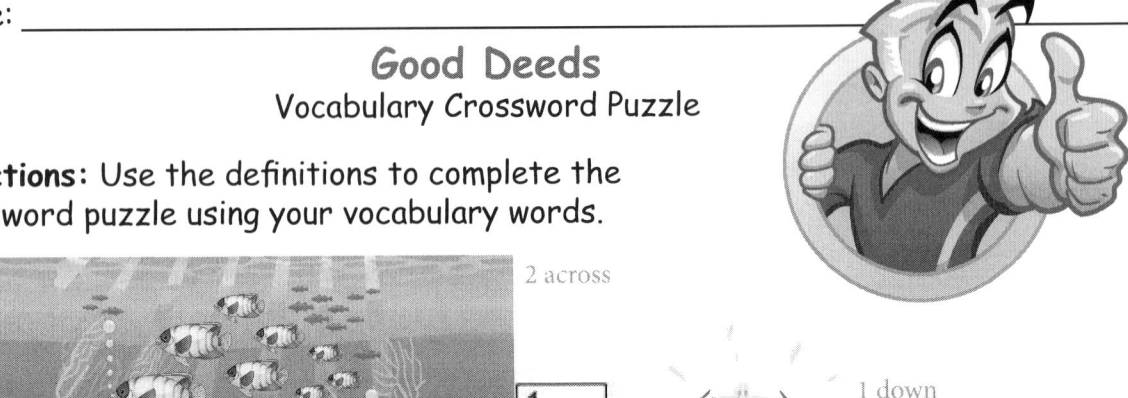

ACROSS:
2 - to follow as a pattern, model, or example
4 - being at the other end, side, or corner
5 - a particular feeling or way of thinking about something
6 - pay no attention to

DOWN:
1 - easily or strongly affected or hurt
3 - moving or changing slightly

17

20.3 - Good Deeds

Name: _____

GOOD DEEDS
Spelling Worksheet

Directions:
Fill in the blanks with an er or or to correctly spell each word.

1. tract ____ ____
2. moth ____ ____
3. rum ____ ____
4. weath ____ ____
5. act ____ ____
6. silv ____ ____
7. juni ____ ____
8. min ____ ____
9. show ____ ____
10. fact ____ ____
11. wat ____ ____
12. tut ____ ____
13. fath ____ ____
14. lead ____ ____
15. vis ____ ____
16. wash ____ ____
17. wond ____ ____
18. fav ____ ____

20.4 - Good Deeds

Name: _____

Good Deeds
Writing with Style Worksheet

Directions: Rewrite these sentences below to add more style. Remember to use strong verbs and add more details to make these sentences better.

1.) Billy went to his room.

2.) She ate her lunch.

3.) I saw a dog.

4.) I wore a hat.

5.) The sun came up.

6.) Henry hit the ball.

Name: _____

Handwriting
Practice 2

Directions:
Use the dashed lines to help you form each word. Then, write each word four more times on your own.

| *go* |
| *do* |
| *cog* |
| *cog* |
| *dog* |
| *dog* |

20.4 - Good Deeds

Name _____

SPELLING TEST

Directions: As your teacher reads your words, write each spelling word on the blanks below. Depending on the lesson, you may have fewer words than spaces below.

1) _____
2) _____
3) _____
4) _____
5) _____
6) _____
7) _____
8) _____
9) _____
10) _____
11) _____
12) _____

13) _____
14) _____
15) _____
16) _____
17) _____
18) _____
19) _____
20) _____

20.5 - Good Deeds

Name _____

GOOD DEEDS
Independent Reading

Directions: Read your independent reading book for 30 minutes. When you are done, write a summary of what you read.

I read _____ by _____
         (book title)   (author)

for 30 minutes today.

_____   _____
My Signature   Parent/Guardian Signature

Details

Read your independent reading book for 30 minutes. When you are done, write a summary of what you read.

_____
_____
_____
_____
_____
_____
_____

Journal Entry

Name _____

Topic: Making Mistakes

Directions: Think about a time when you made a mistake. What happened and what did you learn from it?

Details:

21.1 - Making Mistakes

Name: _____

Spelling - Making Mistakes

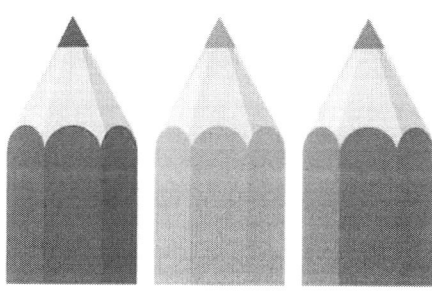

Rainbow Words

Directions:
Please choose three different colored pencils. Write each spelling word three times using each color.

changing _____ _____ _____

swimming _____ _____ _____

taping _____ _____ _____

saving _____ _____ _____

coming _____ _____ _____

tapping _____ _____ _____

grinning _____ _____ _____

falling _____ _____ _____

taking _____ _____ _____

hoping _____ _____ _____

invited _____ _____ _____

stared _____ _____ _____

wrapped _____ _____ _____

planned _____ _____ _____

continued on the next page...

Spelling - Making Mistakes

Rainbow Words

Directions:
Please choose three different colored pencils. Write each spelling word three times using each color.

settled _____ _____ _____

liked   _____ _____ _____

filled   _____ _____ _____

rolled   _____ _____ _____

used   _____ _____ _____

worried _____ _____ _____

Name: _____

Making Mistakes
Handwriting Practice

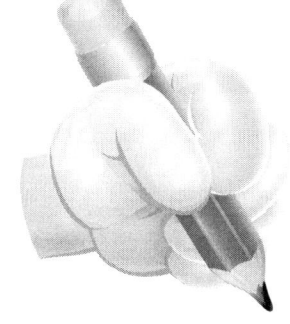

Directions:
Use the dashed lines to help you connect the letters together.

Example:

hththththththththththt

tptptptptptptptptptpt

hphphphphphphphphphp

htphtphtphtphtphtp

htphtphtphtphtphtp

htphtphtphtphtphtp

21.2 - Making Mistakes

Name: _____

Making Mistakes
Vocabulary Crossword Puzzle

Directions:
Use the definitions to complete the crossword puzzle using your vocabulary words.

ACROSS
4 - to charge with a fault and especially with a crime
5 - the state of being friends
6 - to make known (as something wrong)

DOWN
1 - to make a person agree or believe by arguing or showing evidence
2 - a person or thing that stands against another
3 - to support against opposition

Name: _____

Making Mistakes
Spelling Worksheet

Directions:
Write each word again and add the -ed or -ing ending to each word.

1. change = _____
2. swim = _____
3. tape = _____
4. save = _____
5. come = _____
6. tap = _____
7. grin = _____
8. fall = _____
9. take = _____
10. hope = _____

1. invite = _____
2. stare = _____
3. wrap = _____
4. plan = _____
5. settle = _____
6. like = _____
7. fill = _____
8. roll = _____
9. use = _____
10. worry = _____

21.4 - Making Mistakes

Name: _____

Making Mistakes
Adding Content Worksheet

Directions:
Rewrite these paragraphs below to add more content.

I went to the park with my friend yesterday. We swung on the swings. We also played hopscotch. I had a lot of fun.

continued on next page...

Directions:
Rewrite this paragraph below to add more content.

My best friend is great. We spend a lot of time together. We play lots of games and go to lots of different places together. We always have a blast!

21.4 - Making Mistakes

Name: _____

Making Mistakes
Handwriting Practice 2

Directions:
Use the dashed lines to help you form each set of letters. Then, write each set four more times on your own.

ht

hp

pt

ph

th

tp

21.4 - Making Mistakes

Name _____

SPELLING TEST

Directions: As your teacher reads your words, write each spelling word on the blanks below. Depending on the lesson, you may have fewer words than spaces below.

1) _____
2) _____
3) _____
4) _____
5) _____
6) _____
7) _____
8) _____
9) _____
10) _____
11) _____
12) _____

13) _____
14) _____
15) _____
16) _____
17) _____
18) _____
19) _____
20) _____

Name _____

Making Mistakes
Independent Reading

Directions: Read your independent reading book for 30 minutes. When you are done, write a summary of what you read.

I read _____ by _____
       (book title)   (author)

for 30 minutes today.

_____   _____
My Signature   Parent/Guardian Signature

Details

Read your independent reading book for 30 minutes. When you are done, write a summary of what you read.

_____
_____
_____
_____
_____
_____

Journal Entry

Name _____

Topic: Weather Patterns

What is your favorite type of weather? Why?

Details:

22.1 - Weather Patterns

Name: _____

Spelling - Weather Patterns

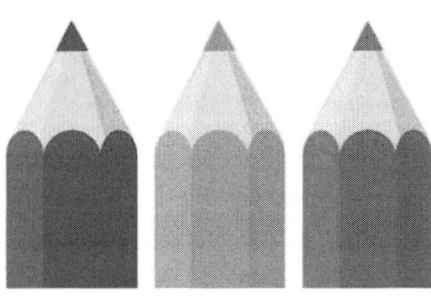

Rainbow Words

Directions:
Please choose three different colored pencils. Write each spelling word three times using each color.

again

answer

been

brought

come

enough

example

father

friend

give

great

kind

most

often

continued on the next page...

35   22.2 - Weather Patterns

Spelling - Weather Patterns

Rainbow Words

Directions:
Please choose three different colored pencils. Write each spelling word three times using each color.

old

once

other

through

where

work

22.2 - Weather Patterns

Name: _____

Weather Patterns
Descriptive Poem Graphic Organizer

Directions: Use this graphic organizer to start brainstorming ideas for your descriptive poem.

Weather Event: _____

Sight – What does this kind of weather look like? What do you see when it happens?

Sound – What does this kind of weather sound like? What do you hear when it happens?

Smell – What does it smell like? What do you smell when this type of weather happens?

continued on next side...

22.2 - Weather Patterns

Touch – How does this type of weather feel on your skin or in the air?

Taste – What does it taste like?
(It's okay if you have trouble with this one. You can compare the taste to something else if you want.)

Weather Patterns
Handwriting Practice

Name _____

Directions:
Use the dashed lines to help you connect the letters together.

Example:

39

22.2 - Weather Patterns

Name: _____

Weather Patterns
Vocabulary Crossword Puzzle

Directions: Use the definitions to complete the crossword puzzle using your vocabulary words.

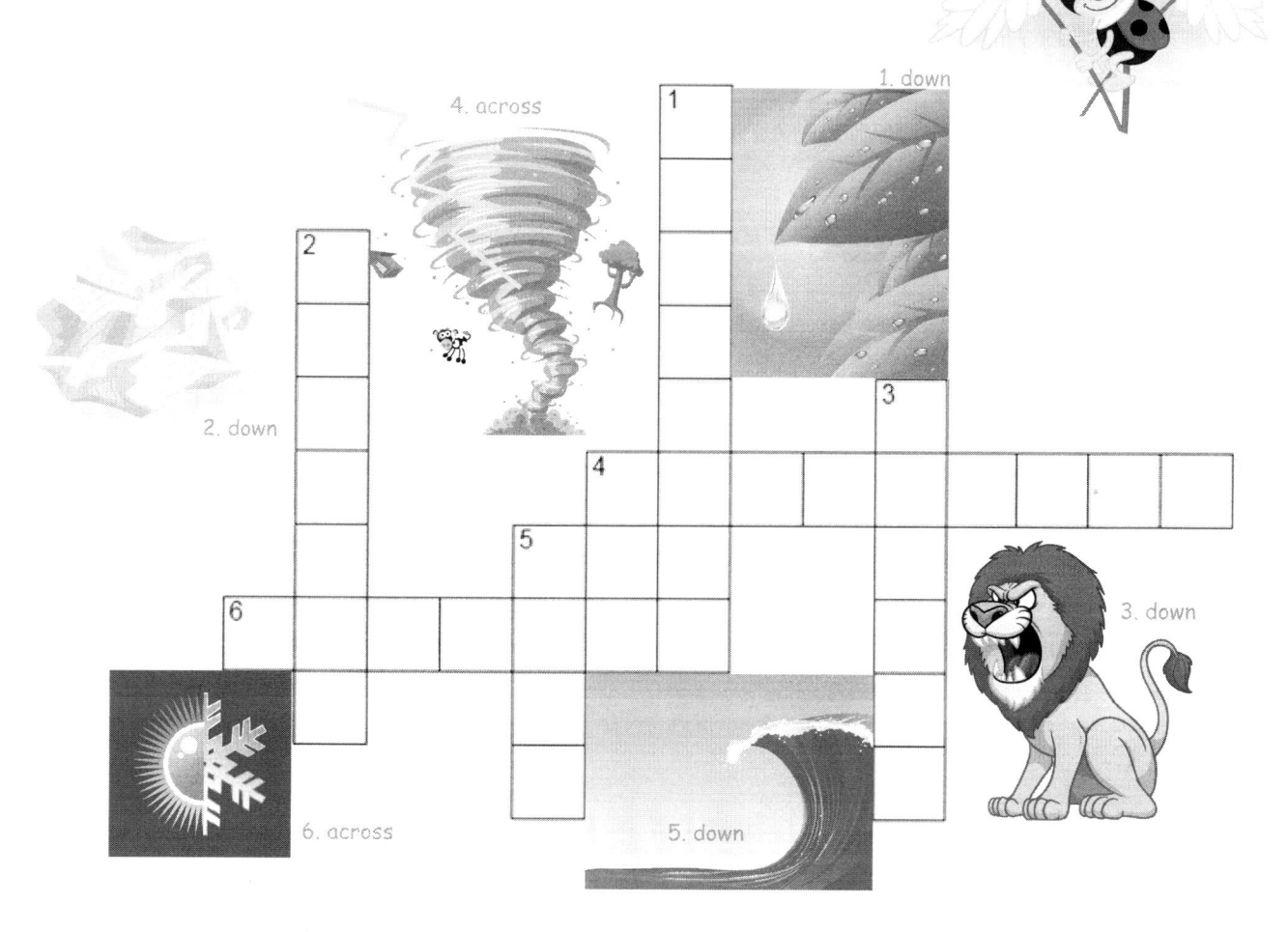

ACROSS:
4. a cyclone formed in the tropics with winds of 74 miles per hour or greater that is usually accompanied by rain, thunder, and lightning
6. a region with specific weather conditions

DOWN:
1. a small amount of liquid that causes wetness
2. to press, bend, or crush out of shape
3. wild or threatening in appearance
5. a moving ridge on the surface of water

22.3 - Weather Patterns

40

Name: _____

Weather Patterns
Spelling Worksheet

Directions: Circle the correct spelling of the word and then write the correct spelling of the word on the blank.

Circle Correct Spelling   Write Correct Word

1. again   agan   agane   _____
2. anser   aswer   answer   _____
3. ben   bein   been   _____
4. brought brout   broght   _____
5. com   come   coum   _____
6. enouf   enugh   enough   _____
7. exampl   example exampel   _____
8. fathur   fathre father   _____
9. friend   frend   freind   _____
10. gieve   give   giev   _____
11. great   grat   graet   _____
12. kiend   kinde   kind   _____
13. most   moust   moste   _____
14. often   oftin   oftne   _____
15. oild   ould   old   _____
16. once   onc   onence   _____
17. othur   other   othre   _____
18. thru   through throgh   _____
19. where   whear   wheare   _____
20. wurk   wourk   work   _____

41   22.4 - Weather Patterns

Name: _____

Weather Patterns
Descriptive Poem Checklist

Directions: Reread your writing carefully. Put a check in each box under Author Check as you complete each item.

Revise and Edit for the following:	
1. SENSORY DETAILS Ask yourself, "Are all five senses used to describe it?" "Could someone who has never experienced this weather event be able to imagine it from my description?" Rewrite parts that need revision.	AUTHOR CHECK:
2. ADJECTIVES Ask yourself, "Are specific and varied adjectives used to describe the weather event?" "Are details used correctly to explain the weather event?" Rewrite parts that need revision.	AUTHOR CHECK:
3. CAPITALIZATION: Use capitals at the beginning of each sentence and for proper nouns. Make corrections if needed.	AUTHOR CHECK:
4. PUNCTUATION: Use periods, exclamation points, and question marks. Make sure commas are used correctly. Make corrections if needed.	AUTHOR CHECK:
5. SPELLING: Check for correct spelling. Make corrections if needed.	AUTHOR CHECK:

22.4 - Weather Patterns

Name: _____

Weather Patterns
Handwriting Practice 2

Directions:
Use the dashed lines to help you form each set of letters. Then, write each set four more times on your own.

Example:

uy

ij

yi

jy

iu

ij

uyj

uyj

43   22.4 - Weather Patterns

Name _____

SPELLING TEST

Directions: As your teacher reads your words, write each spelling word on the blanks below.

1) _____
2) _____
3) _____
4) _____
5) _____
6) _____
7) _____
8) _____
9) _____
10) _____
11) _____
12) _____
13) _____
14) _____
15) _____
16) _____
17) _____
18) _____
19) _____
20) _____

22.5 - Weather Patterns

Name _____

Weather Patterns
Independent Reading

Directions: Read your independent reading book for 30 minutes. When you are done, write a summary of what you read.

I read _____ by _____
      (book title)   (author)

for 30 minutes today.

_____   _____
     My Signature   Parent/Guardian Signature

Details

Read your independent reading book for 30 minutes. When you are done, write a summary of what you read.

_____

_____

_____

_____

_____

_____

_____

Name _____

Natural Disasters Journal Entry

Directions: Write your response to the prompt on the lines below. Don't forget to check for complete sentences as you write.

Prompt: What experience do you have with natural disasters? Have you or someone you know experienced one? Have you seen one on TV or read about one in a book? Explain your experience.

_____
_____
_____
_____
_____
_____
_____
_____
_____
_____
_____
_____
_____
_____
_____

23.1 - Natural Disasters

Name: _____

Spelling - Natural Disasters

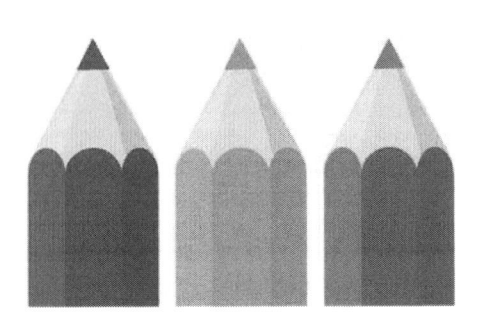

Rainbow Words

Directions:
Please choose three different colored pencils. Write each spelling word three times using each color.

any

both

cold

color

does

earth

eyes

find

four

from

have

learn

listen

many

continued on the next page...

23.2 - Natural Disasters

Spelling - Natural Disasters

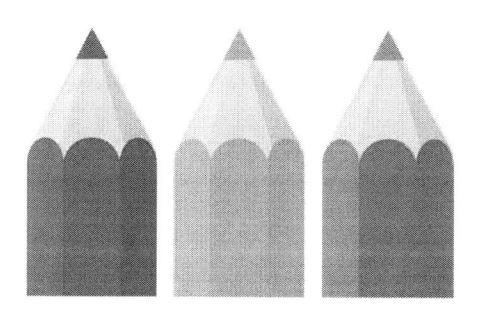

Rainbow Words

Directions:
Please choose three different colored pencils. Write each spelling word three times using each color.

move   _____   _____   _____

only   _____   _____   _____

their   _____   _____   _____

though   _____   _____   _____

want   _____   _____   _____

water   _____   _____   _____

23.2 - Natural Disasters

Name: _____

Natural Disasters
Handwriting Practice 1

Directions:
Use the dashed lines to help you connect the letters together.

Example:

23.2 - Natural Disasters

Name: _____

Natural Disasters
Vocabulary Crossword Puzzle

Directions:
Use the definitions to complete the crossword puzzle using your vocabulary words.

1 down
4 across
3 down
2 across
6 across
5 across

ACROSS:
2.) a severe test or experience
4.) a shaking or trembling of a portion of the earth
5.) a great flow of water that rises and spreads over the land
6.) notice given beforehand especially of danger or evil

DOWN:
1.) a vent in the earth's crust from which melted rock or hot rock and steam come out
3.) a great sea wave produced especially by an earthquake or volcano eruption under the sea

23.3 - Natural Disasters

Name: _____

Natural Disasters
Discussion Graphic Organizer

Directions:
Use this graphic organizer to take notes for your natural disasters discussion.

VOLCANOS

Important Facts	Questions

EARTHQUAKES

Important Facts	Questions

continued on the next page...

TSUNAMIS

Important Facts	Questions

23.3 - Natural Disasters

Name: _____

Natural Disasters
Spelling Worksheet

Directions:
Circle the correct spelling of the spelling word and then write the correct spelling of the word on the blank.

(Circle) Correct Spelling   Write Correct Word

1. any   ani   ane   _____
2. bouth   bothe   both   _____
3. cold   colde   coulde   _____
4. colur   color   culor   _____
5. does   duse   dos   _____
6. erth   eurth   earth   _____
7. ies   eys   eyes   _____
8. find   fiend   finde   _____
9. four   foer   fure   _____
10. frome from   fromm   _____
11. hav   haev   have   _____
12. lern   lurn   learn   _____
13. listen lisen   liesen   _____
14. many   manee   meny   _____
15. muve   mouve   move   _____
16. only   onlee   onle   _____
17. ther   thear   their   _____
18. though thogh   thoug   _____
19. wunt   want   wante   _____
20. water wuter   watre   _____

53   23.4 - Natural Disasters

Name: _____

Natural Disasters
Handwriting Practice 2

Directions:
Use the dashed lines to help you form each set of letters. Then, write each set four more times on your own.

Example:

uy

ij

yi

jy

iu

uj

uyj

uyj

23.4 - Natural Disasters

54

Name _____

SPELLING TEST

Directions: As your teacher reads your words, write each spelling word on the blanks below.

1) _____
2) _____
3) _____
4) _____
5) _____
6) _____
7) _____
8) _____
9) _____
10) _____
11) _____
12) _____
13) _____
14) _____
15) _____
16) _____
17) _____
18) _____
19) _____
20) _____

23.5 - Natural Disasters

Name: _____

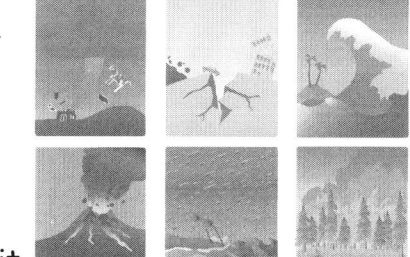

Natural Disasters
Main Idea and Details Graphic Organizer

Directions: Choose one section from "Natural Disasters," and write down the main idea and three details to support it.

Section: _____

Main Idea:

Detail:

Detail:

Detail:

23.5 - Natural Disasters

Name _____

Natural Disasters
Independent Reading

Directions: Read your independent reading book for 30 minutes. When you are done, write a summary of what you read.

I read _____ by _____
   (book title)   (author)

for 30 minutes today.

_____   _____
My Signature   Parent/Guardian Signature

Details

Read your independent reading book for 30 minutes. When you are done, write a summary of what you read.

_____
_____
_____
_____
_____
_____
_____

Name

Glaciers Journal Entry

Directions: Write your response to the prompt on the lines below. Don't forget to check for complete sentences as you write.

Prompt: Write a short story about what's happening in this picture. Use your imagination!

24.1 - Glaciers

Name: _____

Spelling - Glaciers

Rainbow Words

Directions:
Please choose three different colored pencils. Write each spelling word three times using each color.

said   _____   _____   _____

people   _____   _____   _____

they   _____   _____   _____

were   _____   _____   _____

know   _____   _____   _____

would   _____   _____   _____

some   _____   _____   _____

your   _____   _____   _____

because   _____   _____   _____

mother   _____   _____   _____

could   _____   _____   _____

should   _____   _____   _____

whose   _____   _____   _____

you   _____   _____   _____

continued on the next page...

Spelling - Glaciers

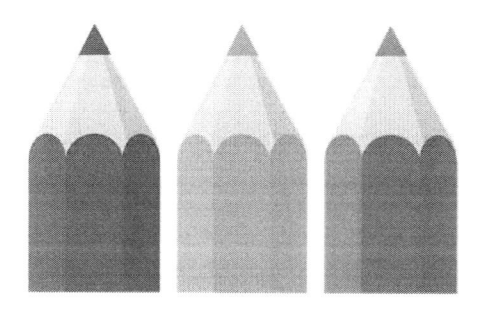

Rainbow Words

Directions:
Please choose three different colored pencils. Write each spelling word three times using each color.

one _____   _____   _____

what _____   _____   _____

put _____   _____   _____

laughed _____   _____   _____

probably _____   _____   _____

favorite _____   _____   _____

Name: _____

Glaciers
Opinion Paragraph Prewrite

Directions:
Do you think that glaciers should be protected and saved? Write your opinion on the line below. Then, list at least two reasons with details.

Opinion: _____

Reason #1: _____

Reason #2: _____

Reason #3: _____

Name: _____

Glaciers
Handwriting Practice 1

Directions:
Use the dashed lines to help you connect the letters together.

Example:

ksksksksksksksksksksks

krkrkrkrkrkrkrkrkrkrk

srsrsrsrsrsrsrsrsrsrsrs

ksksksksksksksksksksks

krkrkrkrkrkrkrkrkrkrk

srsrsrsrsrsrsrsrsrsrsrs

24.2 - Glaciers

Name: _____

Glaciers
Vocabulary Crossword Puzzle

Directions:
Use the definitions to complete the crossword puzzle using your vocabulary words.

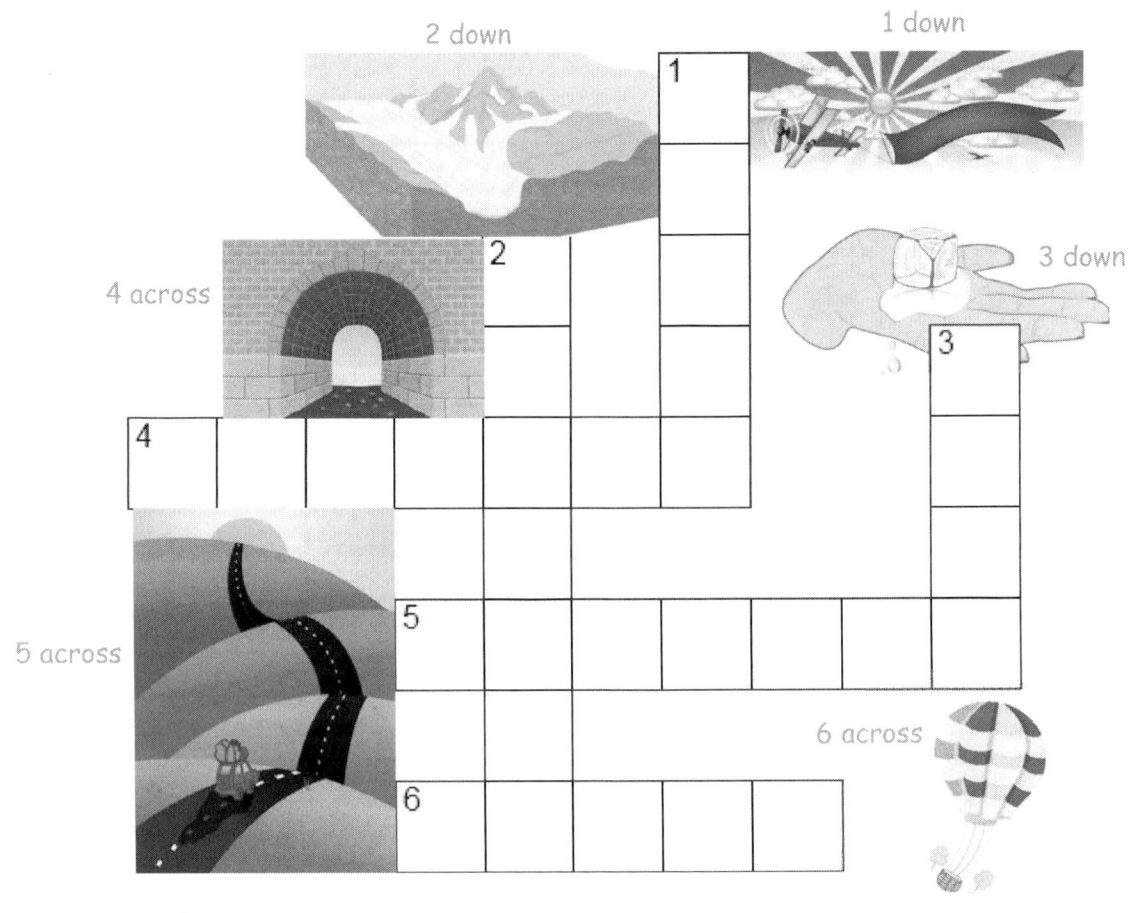

ACROSS:
4) a road, path, channel, or course by which something can pass
5) being at a great distance
6) to move along without effort

DOWN:
1) to move smoothly, silently, and effortlessly
2) a large body of ice moving slowly down a slope or valley or spreading outward on a land surface
3) to change from a solid to a liquid state usually through heat

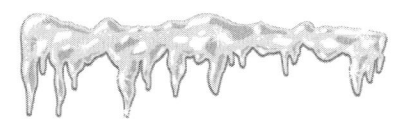

24.3 - Glaciers

Name: _____

Glaciers
Spelling Worksheet

Directions:
Circle the correct spelling of the spelling word and then write the correct spelling of the word on the blank.

(Circle) Correct Spelling   Write Correct Word

1. sead   said   seid   _____
2. peaple   peepol   people   _____
3. thei   they   theiy   _____
4. were   wure   wuer   _____
5. know   knou   nowe   _____
6. wold   would   wolde   _____
7. some   sume   soum   _____
8. yor   your   youre   _____
9. becaus   becaese   because   _____
10. mothur muther   mother   _____
11. coude   could   coulde   _____
12. should sholde   shoud   _____
13. whos   whous   whose   _____
14. you   yoo   yoe   _____
15. one   wone   wonn   _____
16. wat   what   whut   _____
17. put   pud   pute   _____
18. laghed laughed   laufed   _____
19. probably probubly probebly   _____
20. favrite favrote   favorite   _____

24.4 - Glaciers

Name: _____

Glaciers
Opinion Paragraph Checklist

Directions: Reread your writing carefully. Put a check in each box under Author Check as you complete each item.

Revise and Edit for the following:	
1. CLARITY AND MEANING: Ask yourself, "Is your opinion about saving or not saving glaciers clear?" "Are all of your reasons explained and easy to follow?" Rewrite parts that are unclear or need revision.	AUTHOR CHECK:
2. CORRECT USE OF WORDS: Ask yourself, Are specific and varied adjectives and adverbs used?" "Are details used to explain your points?" "Do the sentences sound good together?" Rewrite parts that need revision.	AUTHOR CHECK:
3. CAPITALIZATION: Use capitals at the beginning of each sentence and for proper nouns. Make corrections if needed.	AUTHOR CHECK:
4. PUNCTUATION: Use periods, exclamation points, and question marks. Make sure commas are used correctly. Make corrections if needed.	AUTHOR CHECK:
5. SPELLING: Check for correct spelling. Make corrections if needed.	AUTHOR CHECK:

Name: _____

Glaciers
Handwriting Practice 2

Directions:
Use the dashed lines to help you form each set of letters. Then, write each set four more times on your own.

Example:

ks

kn

sn

sk

nk

ns

nks

24.4 - Glaciers

Name _____

SPELLING TEST

Directions: As your teacher reads your words, write each spelling word on the blanks below.

1) _____
2) _____
3) _____
4) _____
5) _____
6) _____
7) _____
8) _____
9) _____
10) _____
11) _____
12) _____
13) _____
14) _____
15) _____
16) _____
17) _____
18) _____
19) _____
20) _____

24.5 - Glaciers

Name _____

Glaciers
Independent Reading

Directions: Read your independent reading book for 30 minutes. When you are done, write a summary of what you read.

I read _____ by _____
       (book title)   (author)

for 30 minutes today.

_____   _____
   My Signature   Parent/Guardian Signature

Details

Read your independent reading book for 30 minutes. When you are done, write a summary of what you read.

_____
_____
_____
_____
_____
_____

Name

Vacation Days Journal Entry

Directions: Write your response to the prompt on the lines below. Don't forget to check for complete sentences as you write.

Prompt: What was your most memorable vacation day? What did you do and what made it so memorable?

Name: _____

Spelling - Vacation Days

Rainbow Words

Directions:
Please choose three different colored pencils. Write each spelling word three times using each color.

lonely _____ _____ _____

suddenly _____ _____ _____

actually _____ _____ _____

personally _____ _____ _____

especially _____ _____ _____

formally _____ _____ _____

rapidly _____ _____ _____

dangerously _____ _____ _____

tenderly _____ _____ _____

lovely _____ _____ _____

nicely _____ _____ _____

softly _____ _____ _____

quietly _____ _____ _____

exactly _____ _____ _____

continued on the next page...

Spelling - Vacation Days

Rainbow Words

Directions:
Please choose three different colored pencils. Write each spelling word three times using each color.

friendly _____ _____ _____

quickly _____ _____ _____

closely _____ _____ _____

gladly _____ _____ _____

safely _____ _____ _____

finally _____ _____ _____

Name: _____

Vacation Days
Expository Paragraph Prewrite

Directions:
If you could take a vacation anywhere in the world, where would you go? Fill in your reasons and explanations below.

Vacation Spot: _____
_____
_____

Reason #1: _____

Details:	or	Explanations:

continued on the next page...

Reason #2: _____

Details: or   Explanations:

Reason #3: _____

Details: or   Explanations:

25.2 - Vacation Days

Name: _____

Vacation Days
Handwriting Practice 1

Directions:
Use the dashed lines to help you connect the letters together.

Example:

Name: _____

Vacation Days
Vocabulary Crossword Puzzle

Directions: Use the definitions to complete the crossword puzzle using your vocabulary words.

1 down

2 across

4 down

3 down

5 across

6 across

ACROSS:
2 something that causes a strong feeling of excitement
5 the act or process of wearing away by water, wind, or glaciers
6 to look over and examine closely

DOWN:
1 to leap or dive in to water
3 a deep narrow valley with steep sides and often with a stream flowing through it
4 to thoroughly confuse the understanding of something

75   25.3 - Vacation Days

Name: _____

Vacation Days
Spelling Worksheet

Directions:
Circle the correct spelling of the spelling word and then write the correct spelling of the word on the blank.

(Circle) Correct Spelling   Write Correct Word

1. lonely   lonly   lownly   _____
2. sudenly   sudinly   suddenly   _____
3. actully   actualy   actually   _____
4. personally   personaly   persunally   _____
5. especialy   especially   expecially   _____
6. formaly   formally   formuly   _____
7. rapidly   rapedly   rappidly   _____
8. dangerously   dangerusly   dangeruslly   _____
9. tendurly   tendarly   tenderly   _____
10. lovely   lovly   lovlly   _____
11. nicly   niecly   nicely   _____
12. softlly   softly   souftly   _____
13. quietly   quiatly   qwietly   _____
14. exactlly   exaktly   exactly   _____
15. friendly   frendly   freindly   _____
16. quikly   quickly   qwickly   _____
17. closly   clously   closely   _____
18. gladdly   gladely   gladly   _____
19. safly   safely   saifly   _____
20. finally   finaly   fineally   _____

25.4 - Vacation Days

Name: _____

Vacation Days
Expository Paragraph Checklist

Directions: Reread your writing carefully. Put a check in each box under Author Check as you complete each item. Then give your paragraph and checklist to a peer for a peer check.

Revise and Edit for the following:

1. CLARITY AND MEANING:
Ask yourself,
"Is it clear where I would go on my vacation?"
"Are all three of my reasons explained?"
"Did I explain my reasons enough?"
Rewrite parts that are unclear or need revision.

AUTHOR CHECK: PEER CHECK:

2. CORRECT USE OF WORDS:
Ask yourself,
"Are specific and varied adjectives and adverbs used?"
"Are details used to explain my reasons?"
"Do the sentences sound good together?"
Rewrite parts that need revision.

AUTHOR CHECK: PEER CHECK:

3. CAPITALIZATION:
Use capitals at the beginning of each sentence and for proper nouns.
Make corrections if needed.

AUTHOR CHECK: PEER CHECK:

4. PUNCTUATION:
Use periods, exclamation points, and question marks.
Make sure commas are used correctly.
Make corrections if needed.

AUTHOR CHECK: PEER CHECK:

5. SPELLING:
Check for correct spelling.
Make corrections if needed.

AUTHOR CHECK: PEER CHECK:

Name: _____

Vacation Days
Handwriting Practice 2

Directions:
Use the dashed lines to help you form each word.
Then, write each word four more times on your own.

your

bow

wow

wow

bow

wow

25.4 - Vacation Days

Name _____

SPELLING TEST

Directions: As your teacher reads your words, write each spelling word on the blanks below.

1) _____
2) _____
3) _____
4) _____
5) _____
6) _____
7) _____
8) _____
9) _____
10) _____
11) _____
12) _____
13) _____
14) _____
15) _____
16) _____
17) _____
18) _____
19) _____
20) _____

Name _____

Vacation Days
Independent Reading

Directions: Read your independent reading book for 30 minutes. When you are done, write a summary of what you read.

I read _____ by _____
           (book title)   (author)

for 30 minutes today.

_____   _____
My Signature   Parent/Guardian Signature

Details

What is the point of view of your book? How do you know?

_____
_____
_____
_____
_____
_____
_____

25.5 - Vacation Days

Name _____

Rainy Days Journal Entry

Directions: Write your response to the prompt on the lines below. Don't forget to check for complete sentences as you write.

Prompt: What is your favorite thing to do on a rainy day?

_____
_____
_____
_____
_____
_____
_____
_____
_____
_____
_____
_____
_____
_____
_____

26.1 - Rainy Days

Name: _____

Spelling - Rainy Days

Rainbow Words

Directions:
Please choose three different colored pencils. Write each spelling word three times using each color.

total	_____	_____	_____
central	_____	_____	_____
final	_____	_____	_____
signal	_____	_____	_____
actual	_____	_____	_____
trial	_____	_____	_____
equal	_____	_____	_____
general	_____	_____	_____
metal	_____	_____	_____
petal	_____	_____	_____
simple	_____	_____	_____
chuckle	_____	_____	_____
giggle	_____	_____	_____
middle	_____	_____	_____

continued on the next page...

26.2 - Rainy Days

Spelling - Rainy Days

Rainbow Words

Directions:
Please choose three different colored pencils. Write each spelling word three times using each color.

handle _____ _____ _____

candle _____ _____ _____

uncle _____ _____ _____

table _____ _____ _____

staple _____ _____ _____

wiggle _____ _____ _____

Name: _____

Rainy Days Friendly Letter Prewrite

Directions: Complete the graphic organizer below for your friendly letter. The body of your letter doesn't have to be in complete sentences or paragraph form yet. List your ideas and details.

Date:

Greeting:

Body:

Closing:

Name: _____

Rainy Days
Handwriting Practice 1

Directions:
Use the dashed lines to help you connect the letters together.

Example:

am am am am am am

vn vn vn vn vn vn

am am am am am

vm vm vm vm vm

bn bn bn bn bn bn

vm vm vm vm vm

xn xn xn xn xn xn

Name: _____

Rainy Days
Vocabulary Crossword Puzzle

Directions:
Use the definitions to complete the crossword puzzle using your vocabulary words.

ACROSS:
3   to look at or check carefully
4   a room or space just below the roof of a building
5   wealth (money, jewels, or precious metals) stored up or held in reserve
6   a state of unhappiness

DOWN:
1   to look for and find the position of
2   of first rank, importance or value

26.3 - Rainy Days   86

Name: _____

Rainy Days
Spelling Worksheet

Directions:
Fill in the blanks with an "al" or "le" to correctly spell each word.

1. gener____ ____
2. unc____ ____
3. met____ ____
4. centr____ ____
5. cand____ ____
6. tab____ ____
7. fin____ ____
8. stap____ ____
9. hand____ ____
10. sign____ ____

11. tri____ ____
12. gigg____ ____
13. wigg____ ____
14. equ____ ____
15. tot____ ____
16. chuck____ ____
17. simp____ ____
18. pet____ ____
19. midd____ ____
20. actu____ ____

Name: _____

Rainy Days
Friendly Letter Checklist

Directions: Reread your writing carefully. Put a check in each box under Author Check as you complete each item.

Revise and Edit for the following:	
1. CLARITY AND MEANING: Ask yourself, "Is the story or event I'm writing about clear? Is it easy to follow?" "Are enough details included?" "Is there a clear beginning and end to my letter?" Rewrite parts that are unclear or need revision.	AUTHOR CHECK:
2. CORRECT USE OF WORDS: Ask yourself, "Are specific and varied adjectives and adverbs used?" "Are details correctly used to explain the story or event?" "Do the sentences sound good together?" Rewrite parts that need revision.	AUTHOR CHECK:
3. CAPITALIZATION: Use capitals at the beginning of each sentence and for proper nouns. Make corrections if needed.	AUTHOR CHECK:
4. PUNCTUATION: Use periods, exclamation points, and question marks. Make sure commas are used correctly. Make corrections if needed.	AUTHOR CHECK:
5. SPELLING: Check for correct spelling. Make corrections if needed.	AUTHOR CHECK:

Name: _____

Rainy Days
Handwriting Practice 2

Directions:

Use the dashed lines to help you connect the letters together. Then, write each word four more times on your own.

Example:

fan

ton

ram

room

run

clam

son

26.4 - Rainy Days

Name _____

SPELLING TEST

Directions: As your teacher reads your words, write each spelling word on the blanks below.

1) _____
2) _____
3) _____
4) _____
5) _____
6) _____
7) _____
8) _____
9) _____
10) _____
11) _____
12) _____
13) _____
14) _____
15) _____
16) _____
17) _____
18) _____
19) _____
20) _____

26.5 - Rainy Days

Name: _____

Rainy Days
Plot Graphic Organizer

Directions:
Complete the graphic organizer below after reading "Attic Memories."

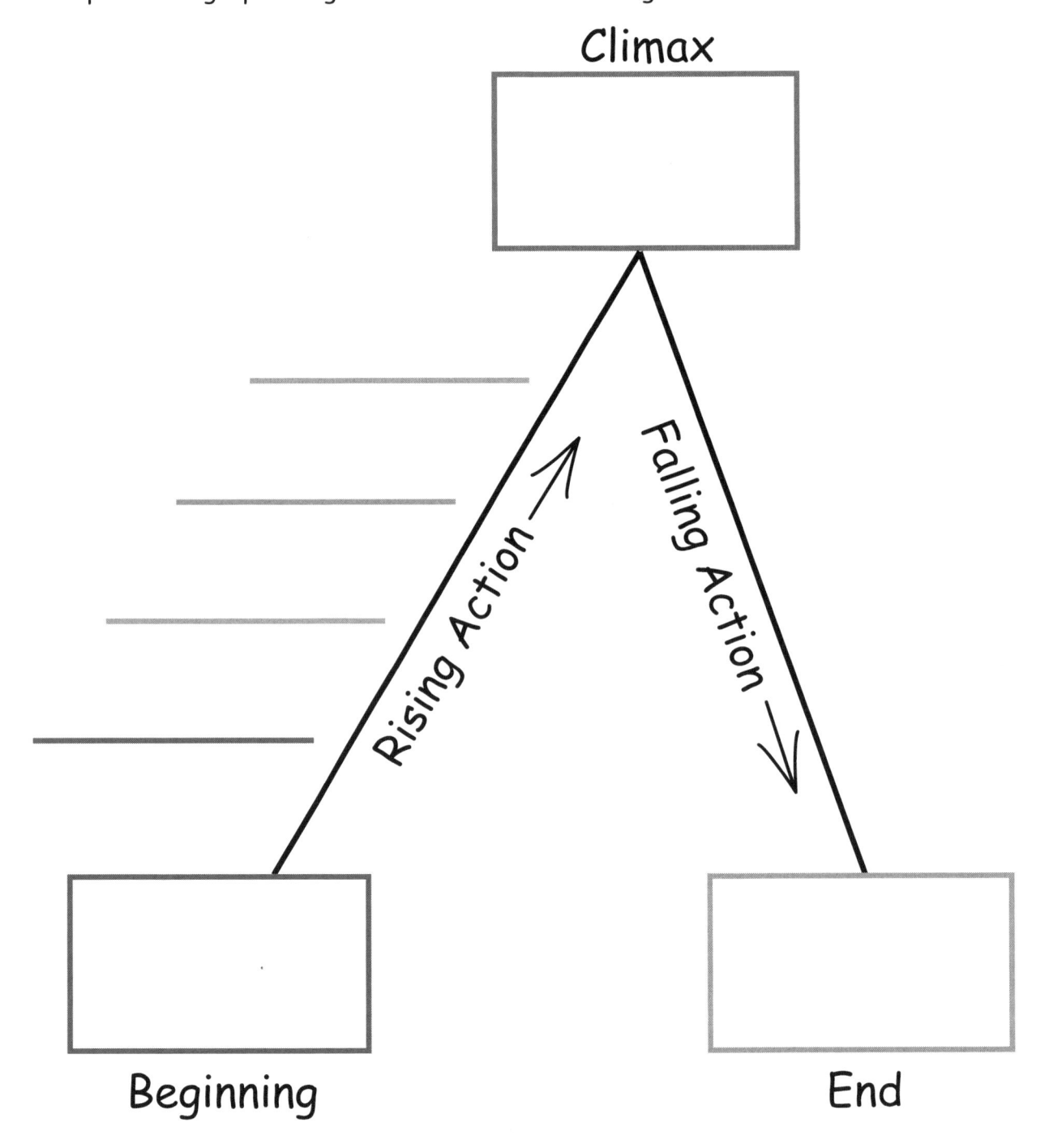

Climax

Rising Action ↗

Falling Action ↘

Beginning

End

91

26.5 - Rainy Days

Name _____

Rainy Days
Independent Reading

Directions: Read your independent reading book for 30 minutes. When you are done, write a short summary of what you read today.

I read _____ by _____
           (book title)   (author)

for 30 minutes today.

_____   _____
      My Signature   Parent/Guardian Signature

Details

Write a short summary of what you read today.

_____
_____
_____
_____
_____
_____
_____

Name _____

Lazy Days Journal Entry

Directions: Write your response to the prompt on the lines below. Don't forget to check for complete sentences as you write.

Prompt: When you have a free day to do whatever you want, what do you like to do?

27.1 - Lazy Days

Name: _____

Spelling - Lazy Days

Rainbow Words

Directions:
Please choose three different colored pencils. Write each spelling word three times using each color.

able _____ _____ _____

apple _____ _____ _____

circle _____ _____ _____

marble _____ _____ _____

juggle _____ _____ _____

pebble _____ _____ _____

rumble _____ _____ _____

waffle _____ _____ _____

twinkle _____ _____ _____

cycle _____ _____ _____

settle _____ _____ _____

double _____ _____ _____

maple _____ _____ _____

ankle _____ _____ _____

continued on the next page...

Spelling - Lazy Days

Rainbow Words

Directions:
Please choose three different colored pencils. Write each spelling word three times using each color.

swivel

squirrel

level

shrivel

label

trowel

Name: _____

Lazy Days
Handwriting Practice 1

Directions:
Use the dashed lines to help you connect the letters together.

Example:

| am am am am am am |

| on on on on on on |

| am am am am am |

| om om om om om |

| bn bn bn bn bn bn |

| vm vm vm vm vm |

| sn sn sn sn sn sn |

27.2 - Lazy Days

Name: _____

Lazy Days
Vocabulary Crossword Puzzle

Directions:
Use the definitions to complete the crossword puzzle using your vocabulary words.

3 across

1 down

4 across

2 down

5 across

6 across

ACROSS:
3 to keep within limits
4 producing or involving action or movement
5 program or agenda
6 remember

DOWN:
1 quiet, tranquil
2 to think about carefully

97

27.3 - Lazy Days

Name: _____

Lazy Days
Spelling Worksheet

Directions:
Fill in the blanks with an "le" or "el" to correctly spell each word.

1. jugg____ ____
2. map____ ____
3. squirr____ ____
4. pebb____ ____
5. waff____ ____
6. ank____ ____
7. app____ ____
8. swiv____ ____
9. twink____ ____
10. marb____ ____
11. lev____ ____
12. sett____ ____
13. doub____ ____
14. rumb____ ____
15. shriv____ ____
16. ab____ ____
17. lab____ ____
18. cyc____ ____
19. trow____ ____
20. circ____ ____

Name: _____

Lazy Days
Handwriting Practice 2

Directions:
Use the dashed lines to help you form each word. Then, write each word four more times on your own.

and

so

but

for

and

so

but

for

27.4 - Lazy Days

Name _____

SPELLING TEST

Directions: As your teacher reads your words, write each spelling word on the blanks below.

1) _____
2) _____
3) _____
4) _____
5) _____
6) _____
7) _____
8) _____
9) _____
10) _____
11) _____
12) _____
13) _____
14) _____
15) _____
16) _____
17) _____
18) _____
19) _____
20) _____

27.5 - Lazy Days

Name: _____

Lazy Days
Revising Writing Worksheet

Directions:
Read the paragraph below. Revise the paragraph using **ARMS** to make it stronger.

I had a silly day at the park yesterday with my dog, Daisy. We didn't get home until late. We walked to our usual neighborhood park, but there were lots of new dogs there. Daisy was excited. She took a swim in the stream. She ran laps around the field with another dog, Axel. What a day!

Updated Paragraph with Revisions:

Name _____

Lazy Days
Independent Reading

Directions: Read your independent reading book for 30 minutes. When you are done, write about the conflict in your story.

I read _____ by _____
         (book title)   (author)

for 30 minutes today.

_____   _____
      My Signature   Parent/Guardian Signature

Details

Write about the conflict in your story. If you haven't reached the conflict in your story yet, please write about the conflict in the last independent reading book you read.

_____
_____
_____
_____
_____
_____

27.5 - Lazy Days

Name: _____

Artists - Journal Entry

Directions: Write your response to the prompt on the lines below. Don't forget to check for complete sentences as you write.

Prompt: What do you enjoy about art?

_____
_____
_____
_____
_____
_____
_____
_____
_____
_____
_____
_____
_____
_____
_____

Name: _____

Spelling - Artists

Rainbow Words

Directions:
Please choose three different colored pencils. Write each spelling word three times using each color.

confusion   _____   _____   _____

version   _____   _____   _____

revision   _____   _____   _____

division   _____   _____   _____

permission   _____   _____   _____

confession   _____   _____   _____

vision   _____   _____   _____

quotation   _____   _____   _____

nation   _____   _____   _____

combination   _____   _____   _____

question   _____   _____   _____

attention   _____   _____   _____

position   _____   _____   _____

action   _____   _____   _____

continued on the next page...

Spelling - Artists

Rainbow Words

Directions:
Please choose three different colored pencils. Write each spelling word three times using each color.

immature

puncture

structure

departure

vulture

capture

Name: _____

Artists
Problem and Solution Paragraph Prewrite

Directions: Describe your problem, how you worked to fix it, and your solution below.

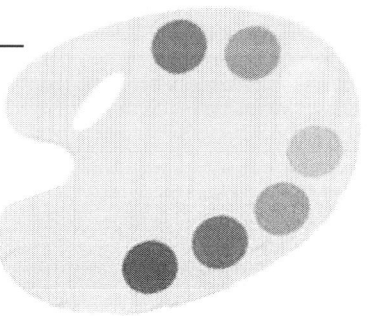

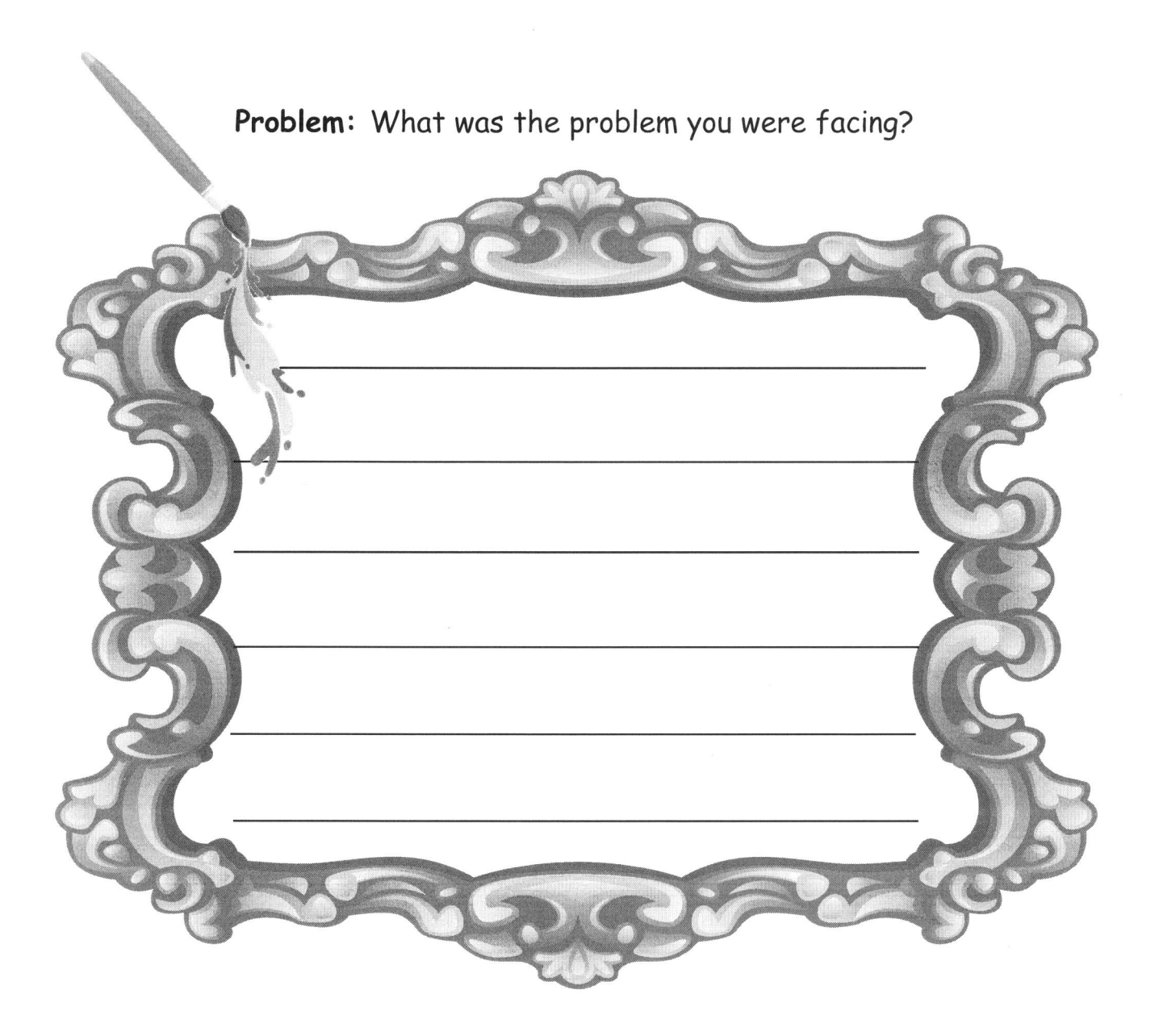

Problem: What was the problem you were facing?

_____

_____

_____

_____

_____

continued on the next page:

Action Steps: What steps were taken to solve the problem?

1. _____

2. _____

3. _____

Solution: How was the problem solved?

Name: _____

Artists - Handwriting Practice 1

Directions: Use the dashed lines to help you connect each set of letters together.

me me me me me

she she she she she

him him him him

it's it's it's it's it's

me me me me me

she she she she she

him him him him

it's it's it's it's it's

28.2 - Artists

Name: _____

Artists
Vocabulary Crossword Puzzle

Directions: Use the definitions to complete the crossword puzzle using your vocabulary words.

ACROSS:
4. a work done with great skill
5. standing out in a very noticeable way

DOWN:
1. very uncommon
2. a building or part of a building in which objects of lasting interest or value are displayed
3. a person skilled in one of the arts
4. applied to and made part of a wall surface

Name: _____

Artists
Spelling Worksheet

Directions: Fill in the blanks with –sion, –tion, or –ture to correctly spell each word.

1. atten ____ ____ ____ ____

2. vi ____ ____ ____ ____

3. depar ____ ____ ____

4. quota ____ ____ ____ ____

5. vul ____ ____ ____ ____

6. ver ____ ____ ____ ____

7. posi ____ ____ ____ ____

8. cap ____ ____ ____ ____

9. revi ____ ____ ____ ____

10. confes ____ ____ ____

11. imma ____ ____ ____ ____

12. divi ____ ____ ____ ____

13. ques ____ ____ ____ ____

14. struc ____ ____ ____ ____

15. na ____ ____ ____ ____

16. confu ____ ____ ____ ____

17. punc ____ ____ ____ ____

18. ac ____ ____ ____ ____

19. combina ____ ____ ____ ____

20. permis____ ____ ____ ____

28.4 - Artists

Name: _____

Artists
Problem and Solution Paragraph Checklist

Directions: Reread your writing carefully. Put a check in each box under Author Check as you complete each item.

Revise and Edit for the following:

1. CLARITY AND MEANING:
Ask yourself,
"Is the problem I'm writing about clear? Is it easy to identify?"
"Are the steps I took to try to solve the problem clear?
Are enough details used?"
"Is the solution to the problem clear?"
Rewrite parts that are unclear or need revision.

AUTHOR CHECK:

2. CORRECT USE OF WORDS:
Ask yourself,
"Are specific and varied adjectives and adverbs used?"
"Are details correctly used to explain the problem and solution?"
"Do the sentences sound good together?"
Rewrite parts that need revision.

AUTHOR CHECK:

3. CAPITALIZATION:
Use capitals at the beginning of each sentence and for proper nouns.
Make corrections if needed.

AUTHOR CHECK:

4. PUNCTUATION:
Use periods, exclamation points, and question marks.
Make sure commas and apostrophes are used correctly.
Make corrections if needed.

AUTHOR CHECK:

5. SPELLING:
Check for correct spelling.
Make corrections if needed.

AUTHOR CHECK:

Name: _____

Artists - Handwriting Practice 2

Directions:
Use the dashed lines to help you form each word. Then, write each word four more times on your own.

me me me me me

she she she she she

him him him him

it's it's it's it's it's

me me me me me

she she she she she

him him him him

it's it's it's it's it's

28.4 - Artists

Name _____

SPELLING TEST

Directions: As your teacher reads your words, write each spelling word on the blanks below.

1) _____
2) _____
3) _____
4) _____
5) _____
6) _____
7) _____
8) _____
9) _____
10) _____
11) _____
12) _____
13) _____
14) _____
15) _____
16) _____
17) _____
18) _____
19) _____
20) _____

Name: _____

Artists
Problem and Solution Worksheet

Directions: Identify the problem and solution from "A Discovery in a Cave."

PROBLEM:	SOLUTION:

Name _____

Artists
Independent Reading

Directions: Read your independent reading book for 30 minutes. When you are done, write a short summary of what you've read.

I read _____ by _____
　　　　　(book title)　　　　　　　　　　　　(author)

for 30 minutes today.

_____　　　　　_____
My Signature　　　　　　　　　　　Parent/Guardian Signature

Details

Write a short summary of what you read today.

_____

_____

_____

_____

_____

_____

_____

Name: _____

Musicians - Journal Entry

Directions: Write your response to the prompt on the lines below. Don't forget to check for complete sentences as you write.

Prompt: What do you enjoy about music? Do you have a favorite musician or song?

29.1 - Musicians

Name: _____

Spelling - Musicians

Rainbow Words

Directions:
Please choose three different colored pencils. Write each spelling word three times using each color.

caught   _____   _____   _____

daughter   _____   _____   _____

laugh   _____   _____   _____

laughter   _____   _____   _____

taught   _____   _____   _____

bought   _____   _____   _____

cough   _____   _____   _____

dough   _____   _____   _____

enough   _____   _____   _____

fought   _____   _____   _____

rough   _____   _____   _____

thought   _____   _____   _____

tough   _____   _____   _____

through   _____   _____   _____

continued on the next page...

Spelling - Musicians

Rainbow Words

Directions:
Please choose three different colored pencils. Write each spelling word three times using each color.

instrument _____ _____ _____

musician _____ _____ _____

popular _____ _____ _____

talent _____ _____ _____

celebrate _____ _____ _____

tradition _____ _____ _____

Name: _____

Musicians
Cause and Effect Paragraph Graphic Organizer

Directions:
Describe the event that you are writing about. Explain what happened to you in the "Cause" box and explain the effects it had in the "Effect" boxes.

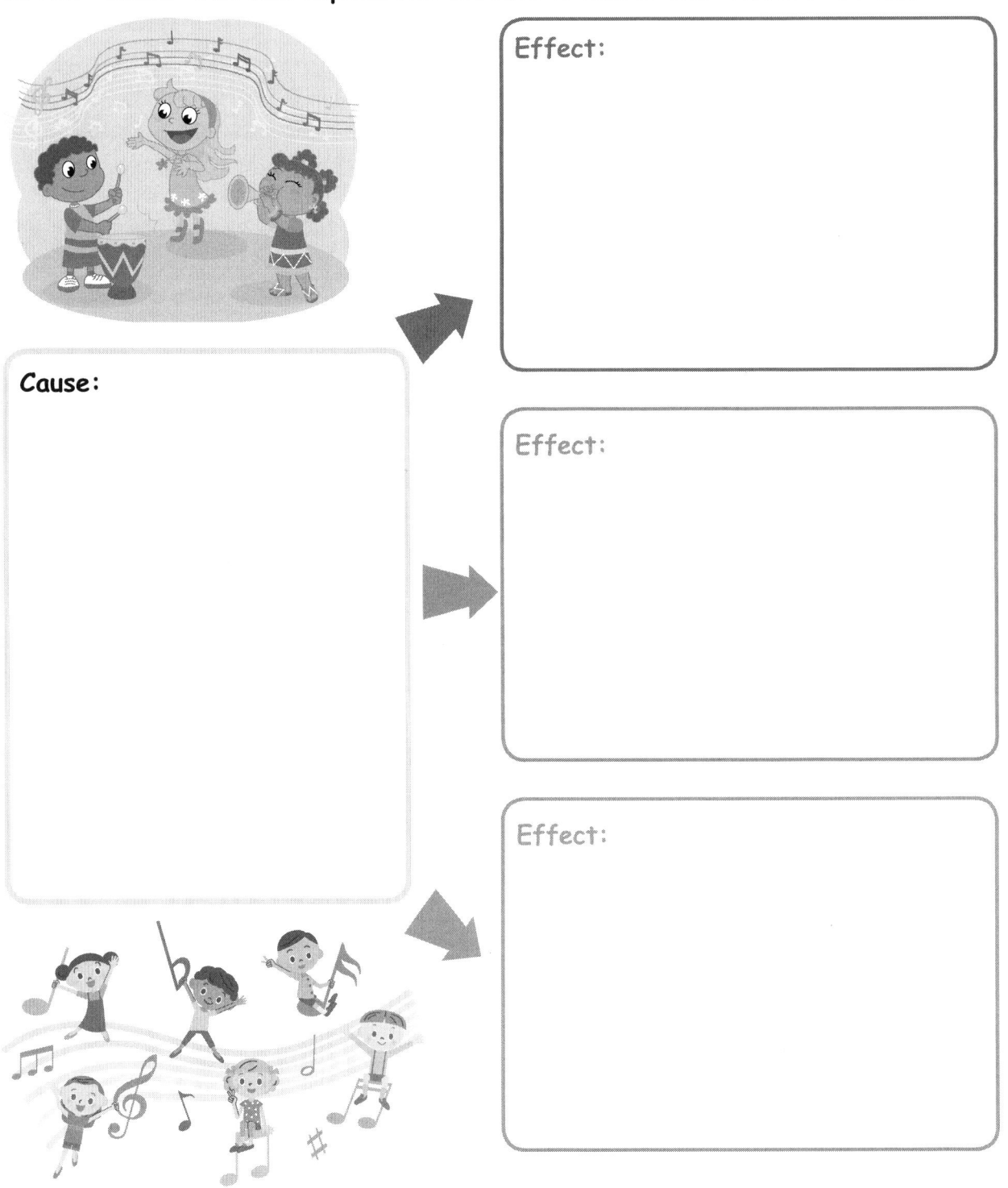

Cause:

Effect:

Effect:

Effect:

119 29.2 - Musicians

Name: _____

Musicians
Handwriting Practice 1

Directions:
Use the dashed lines to help you connect the letters together.

Example:

| can can can can |
| we we we we we we |
| have have have |
| is is is is is is is |
| can can can can |
| we we we we we we |
| have have have |
| is is is is is is is |

29.2 - Musicians

120

Name: _____

Musicians
Vocabulary Crossword Puzzle

Directions: Use the definitions to complete the crossword puzzle using your vocabulary words.

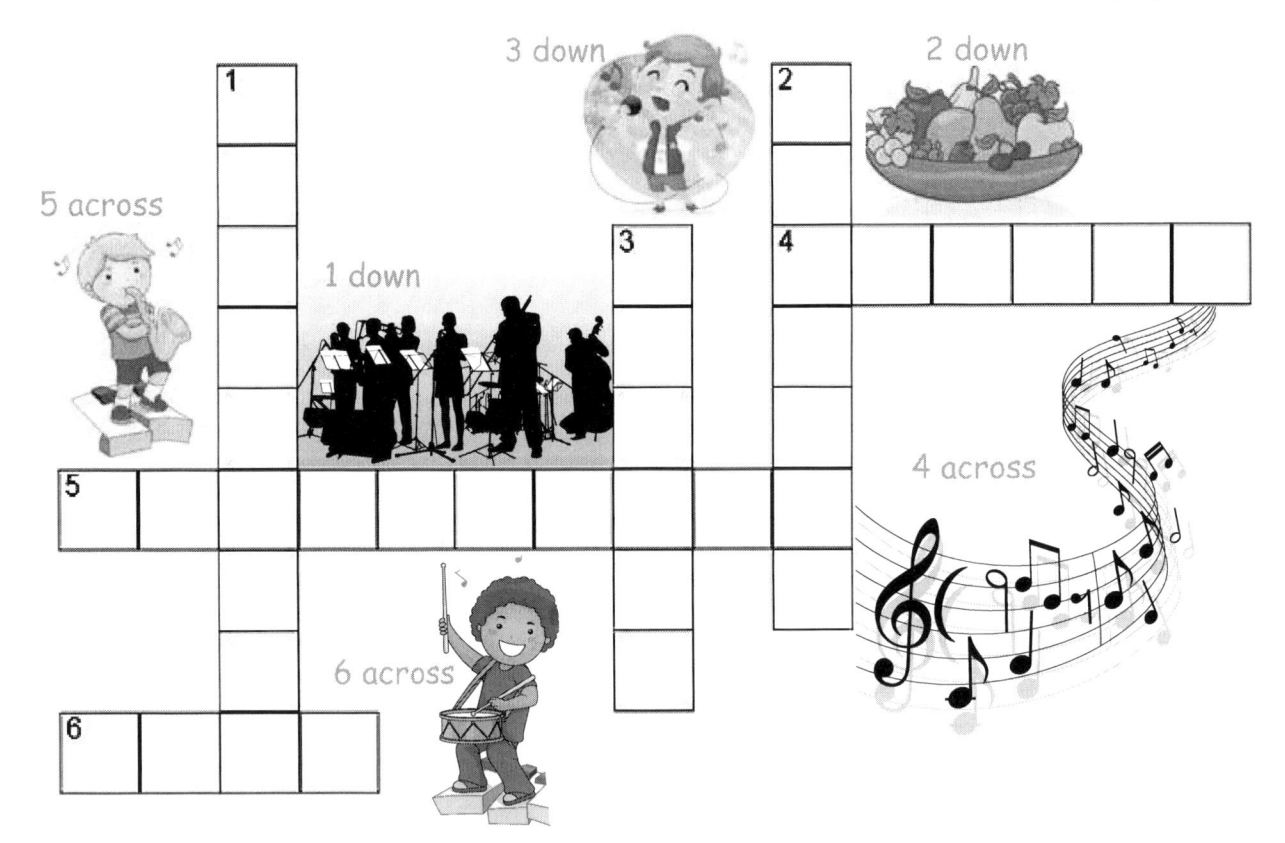

ACROSS:
4. a flow of sound in music having regular accented beats
5. a device used to produce music
6. a rhythmic stress in poetry or music

DOWN:
1. a group of musicians who perform instrumental music using mostly stringed instruments
2. a number or collection of different things
3. the natural abilities of a person

Name: _____

Musicians
Spelling Worksheet

Directions:
Circle the correct spelling of the spelling word and then write the correct spelling of the word on the blank.

Circle Correct Spelling: **Write Correct Word:**

1. laughter   loughter   lafter   _____
2. musican   musician   musicane   _____
3. talente   talent   talant   _____
4. populer   populre   popular   _____
5. cought   caught   caute   _____
6. instrument   instrumint   instrumant   _____
7. tought   taute   taught   _____
8. daughter   doughter   dauter   _____
9. thru   through   thraugh   _____
10. laugh   lough   laghe   _____
11. baute   baught   bought   _____
12. fought   faught   faute   _____
13. celibrate   celebrate   celebaet   _____
14. raugh   rough   rugh   _____
15. enugh   enaugh   enough   _____
16. tradition   tradision   tradishon   _____
17. tuff   taugh   tough   _____
18. doghe   dough   daugh   _____
19. thought   thaught   thoght   _____
20. cough   caugh   caufe   _____

29.4 - Musicians   122

Name: _____

Musicians
Cause and Effect Paragraph Checklist

Directions: Reread your writing carefully. Put a check in each box under Author Check as you complete each item.

Revise and Edit for the following:

1. CLARITY AND MEANING:
Ask yourself,
"Is the story I'm telling clear?"
"Is it easy to identify the cause and effect?"
"Are enough details used?"
Rewrite parts that are unclear or need revision.

AUTHOR CHECK:

2. CORRECT USE OF WORDS:
Ask yourself,
"Are specific and varied adjectives and adverbs used?"
"Are details correctly used to explain the cause and effect?"
"Do the sentences sound good together?"
Rewrite parts that need revision.

AUTHOR CHECK:

3. CAPITALIZATION:
Use capitals at the beginning of each sentence and for proper nouns.
Make corrections if needed.

AUTHOR CHECK:

4. PUNCTUATION:
Use periods, exclamation points, and question marks.
Make sure commas and apostrophes are used correctly.
Make corrections if needed.

AUTHOR CHECK:

5. SPELLING:
Check for correct spelling.
Make corrections if needed.

AUTHOR CHECK:

Name: _____

Musicians
Handwriting Practice 2

Directions:
Use the dashed lines to help you form each word. Then, write each word four more times on your own.

can

we

have

is

can

we

have

is

29.4 - Musicians

Name _____

SPELLING TEST

Directions: As your teacher reads your words, write each spelling word on the blanks below.

1) _____
2) _____
3) _____
4) _____
5) _____
6) _____
7) _____
8) _____
9) _____
10) _____
11) _____
12) _____
13) _____
14) _____
15) _____
16) _____
17) _____
18) _____
19) _____
20) _____

Name _____

Musicians
Independent Reading

Directions: Read your independent reading book for 30 minutes. When you are done, write a short summary of what you've read.

I read _____ by _____
           (book title)   (author)

for 30 minutes today.

_____   _____
    My Signature   Parent/Guardian Signature

Details

Write a short summary of what you read today.

_____
_____
_____
_____
_____
_____
_____

Name: _____

Athletes - Journal Entry

Directions: Write your response to the prompt on the lines below. Don't forget to check for complete sentences as you write.

Prompt:
What is your favorite sport to watch or play? Why?

_____
_____
_____
_____
_____
_____
_____
_____
_____
_____
_____
_____
_____
_____
_____

Name: _____

Spelling - Athletes

Rainbow Words

Directions:
Please choose three different colored pencils. Write each spelling word three times using each color.

afternoon _____ _____ _____

without _____ _____ _____

airplane _____ _____ _____

homework _____ _____ _____

birthday _____ _____ _____

sometimes _____ _____ _____

himself _____ _____ _____

something _____ _____ _____

faraway _____ _____ _____

everything _____ _____ _____

anyone _____ _____ _____

dishwasher _____ _____ _____

notebook _____ _____ _____

football _____ _____ _____

continued on the next page...

Spelling - Athletes

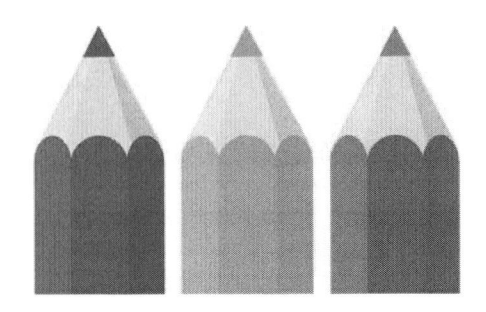

Rainbow Words

Directions:
Please choose three different colored pencils. Write each spelling word three times using each color.

hallway _____ _____ _____

sunset _____ _____ _____

everyone _____ _____ _____

upstairs _____ _____ _____

outdoors _____ _____ _____

sunshine _____ _____ _____

Name: _____

Athletes
Compare and Contrast Paragraph Graphic Organizer

Directions: Compare and contrast your two sports below. Write at least two details in each section of the Venn diagram.

Sport One: _____   Sport Two: _____

30.2 - Athletes   130

Name: _____

Athletes
Handwriting Practice 1

Directions:
Use the dashed lines to help you form each word.

find find find

give give give give

just just just just

kick kick kick kick

find find find

give give give give

just just just just

kick kick kick kick

Name: _____

Athletes
Vocabulary Crossword Puzzle

Directions:
Use the definitions to complete the crossword puzzle using your vocabulary words.

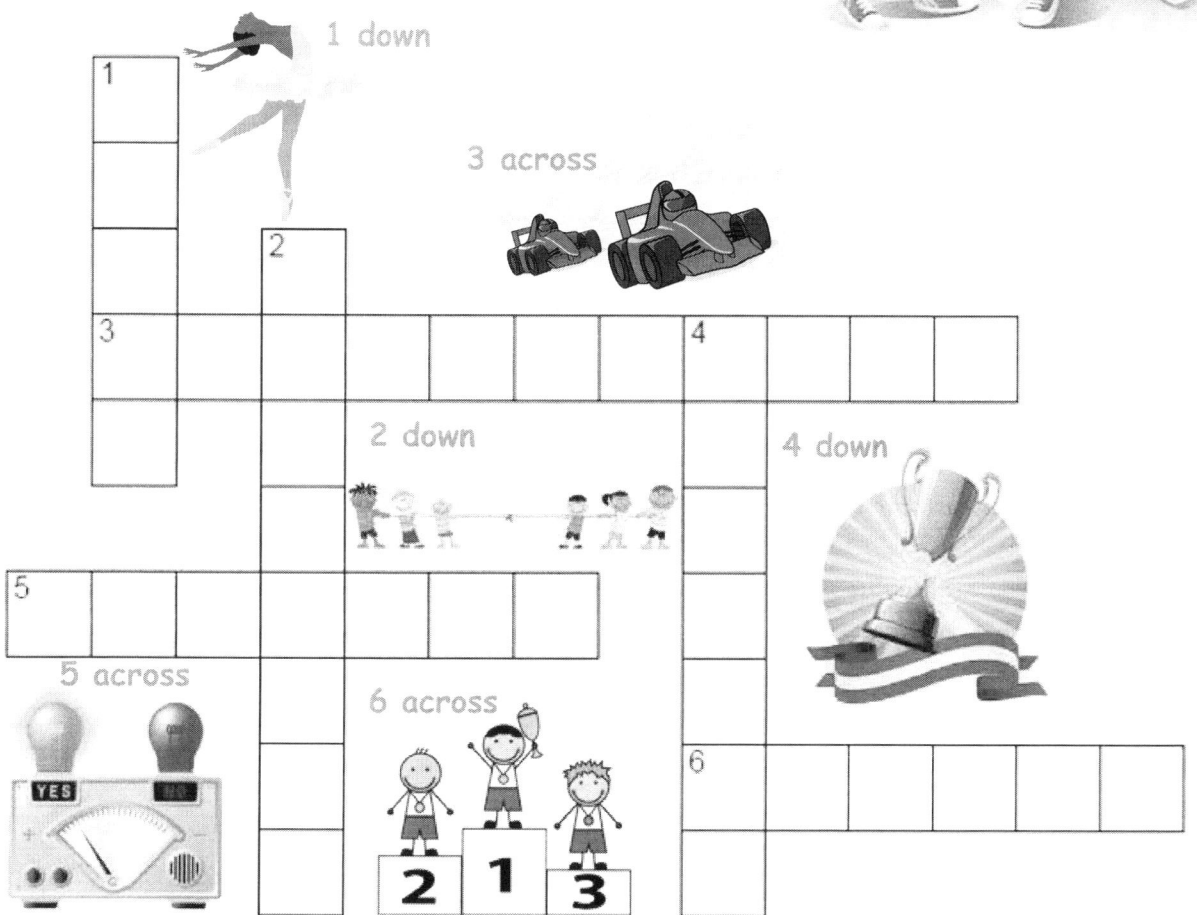

ACROSS:
3. a contest between rivals
5. not to be doubted
6. a raised platform

DOWN:
1. ease of movement
2. an eager desire for social standing, fame, or power
4. to gain victory or win

30.3 - Athletes

132

Name: _____

Athletes
Spelling Worksheet

Directions:
Circle the correct spelling of the spelling word and then write the correct spelling of the word on the blank.

(Circle) **Correct Spelling:**   **Write Correct Word:**

1. afternon   afternoun   afternoon   _____
2. without   wethout   witout   _____
3. airplain   airplane   airplan   _____
4. homwork   homework   homewurk   _____
5. burthday   birthdae   birthday   _____
6. sometimes   somtimes   sumtimes   _____
7. himself   himselfe   himmself   _____
8. someting   somthing   something   _____
9. faraway   fareaway   farawae   _____
10. everything everething   evrything   _____
11. anyon   anyone   aneone   _____
12. dishwashur dishwaser   dishwasher   _____
13. notebook   notbook   noteboke   _____
14. footbal   fotball   football   _____
15. halway   hallway   hallwae   _____
16. sunset   sunsett   sonset   _____
17. everyone   evereone   evryone   _____
18. upstares   upstairs   upstaers   _____
19. outdors   outdours   outdoors   _____
20. sunshin   sunshien   sunshine   _____

Name: _____

Athletes
Cause and Effect Paragraph Checklist

Directions: Reread your writing carefully. Put a check in each box under Author Check as you complete each item.

Revise and Edit for the following:

1. CLARITY AND MEANING:
Ask yourself,
"Is it clear what two sports I am comparing and contrasting?"
"Is it clear to see what they have in common?"
"Are their differences easy to identify?"
Rewrite parts that are unclear or need revision.

AUTHOR CHECK:

2. CORRECT USE OF WORDS:
Ask yourself,
"Are specific and varied adjectives and adverbs used?"
"Are details used to explain the similarities and differences?"
"Do the sentences sound good together?"
Rewrite parts that need revision.

AUTHOR CHECK:

3. CAPITALIZATION:
Use capitals at the beginning of each sentence and for proper nouns. Make corrections if needed.

AUTHOR CHECK:

4. PUNCTUATION:
Use periods, exclamation points, and question marks.
Make sure commas and apostrophes are used correctly.
Make corrections if needed.

AUTHOR CHECK:

5. SPELLING:
Check for correct spelling.
Make corrections if needed.

AUTHOR CHECK:

Name: _____

Athletes
Handwriting Practice 2

Directions:
Use the dashed lines to help you form each word. Then, write each word four more times on your own.

find

give

just

kick

find

give

just

kick

30.4 - Athletes

Name _____

SPELLING TEST

Directions: As your teacher reads your words, write each spelling word on the blanks below.

1) _____
2) _____
3) _____
4) _____
5) _____
6) _____
7) _____
8) _____
9) _____
10) _____
11) _____
12) _____
13) _____
14) _____
15) _____
16) _____
17) _____
18) _____
19) _____
20) _____

30.5 - Athletes

Name: _____

Athletes
Compare and Contrast Worksheet

Directions:
Choose two athletes from "Olympic Athletes" and compare and contrast them on the Venn diagram below.

Athlete One: _____   Athlete Two: _____

137

30.5 - Athletes

Name _____

Athletes
Independent Reading

Directions: Read your independent reading book for 30 minutes. When you are done, compare and contrast two characters in the story or compare and contrast this book to another you have recently read.

I read _____ by _____
           (book title)   (author)

for 30 minutes today.

_____   _____
     My Signature   Parent/Guardian Signature

Details

What are you comparing and contrasting?

_____

_____

Compare:

_____

_____

Contrast:

_____

_____

30.5 - Athletes

Name: _____

Rolling Objects - Journal Entry

Directions: Write your response to the prompt on the lines below. Don't forget to check for complete sentences as you write.

Prompt: How would your life be different if the wheel had not been invented?

_____
_____
_____
_____
_____
_____
_____
_____
_____
_____
_____
_____
_____

Name: _____

Spelling - Rolling Objects

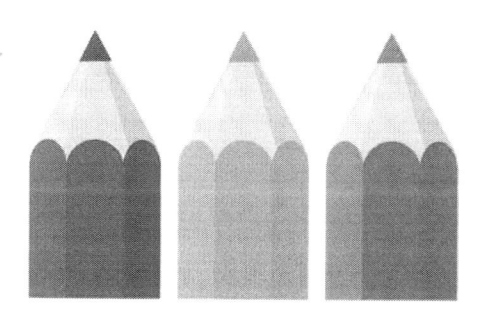

Rainbow Words

Directions:
Please choose three different colored pencils. Write each spelling word three times using each color.

hugged _____ _____ _____

correct _____ _____ _____

funny _____ _____ _____

happy _____ _____ _____

puppy _____ _____ _____

common _____ _____ _____

collect _____ _____ _____

bottles _____ _____ _____

different _____ _____ _____

lesson _____ _____ _____

error _____ _____ _____

pulled _____ _____ _____

begged _____ _____ _____

silly _____ _____ _____

continued on the next page...

Spelling - Rolling Objects

Rainbow Words

Directions:
Please choose three different colored pencils. Write each spelling word three times using each color.

matter　_____　_____　_____

supper　_____　_____　_____

setting　_____　_____　_____

jelly　_____　_____　_____

ladder　_____　_____　_____

tunnel　_____　_____　_____

Name: _____

Rolling Objects
Informational Paragraph Graphic Organizer

Directions: Follow these steps to choose a topic and plan your research.

Step 1: First, narrow your topic down to two inventions that you might want to write about. List two inventions that you think might interest your classmates as well as yourself.

Invention 1: _____

Invention 2: _____

Step 2: Next, write some questions that show what you would like to know about each of these inventions. These are questions you will try to answer when you do research.

3 Questions about Invention 1:

1: _____
2: _____
3: _____

3 Questions about Invention 2:

1: _____
2: _____
3: _____

31.2 - Rolling Objects

Name: _____

Step 3: Choose ONE of the topics above, and search for information about that topic online, in a library, or in your classroom. Each time you find a source of information about the topic, ask yourself if that source will answer your questions. If it will not, put it back and look for another source that will. (If you find other information that is very interesting, write that down too.)

Step 4: Write down the information you find about your invention. Be sure to write the facts in your own words. (Don't copy the information word for word from the place where you found it.) Find three major facts about the invention and list two or three details that tell more about each fact.

Invention: _____

Fact 1: _____
_____

    Detail: _____
    Detail: _____
    Detail: _____

Fact 2: _____
_____

    Detail: _____
    Detail: _____
    Detail: _____

Fact 3: _____
_____

    Detail: _____
    Detail: _____
    Detail: _____

Name: _____

Rolling Objects
Handwriting Practice 1

Directions:
Use the dashed lines to help you connect the letters together.

Example:

love love love love

put put put put put

quick quick quick

ray ray ray ray ray

love love love love

put put put put put

quick quick quick

ray ray ray ray ray

31.2 - Rolling Objects

Name: _____

Rolling Objects
Vocabulary Crossword Puzzle

Directions: Use the definitions to complete the crossword puzzle using your vocabulary words.

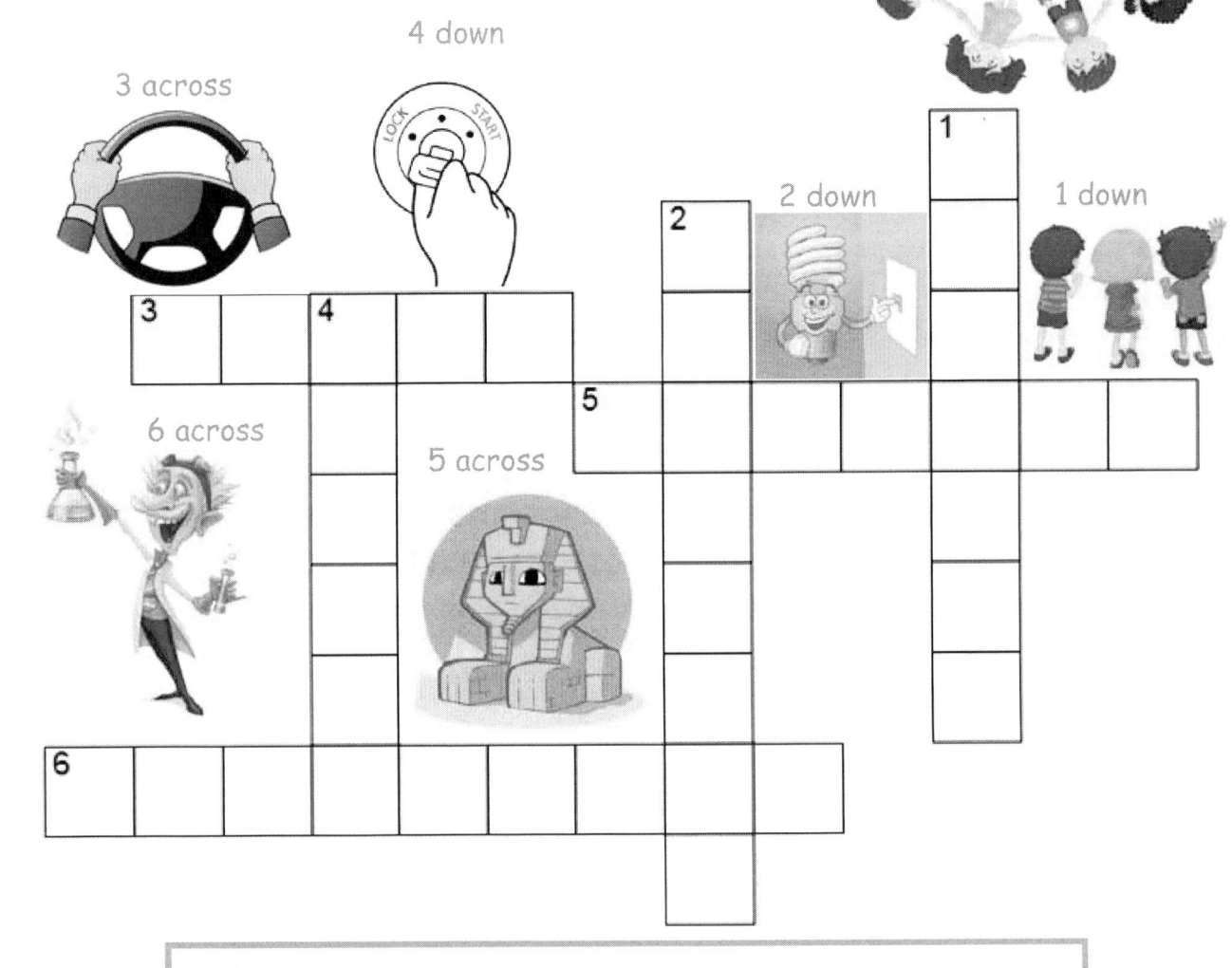

3 across
4 down
2 down
1 down
6 across
5 across

ACROSS
3. to direct the course or the course of
5. of or relating to a period of time long past
6. something thought up or created

DOWN
1. bringing about backward movement
2. the particular purpose for which something is used
4. to make able

145   31.3 - Rolling Objects

Name: _____

Rolling Objects
Spelling Worksheet

Directions:
Circle the correct spelling of the spelling word and then write the correct spelling of the word on the blank.

Circle Correct Spelling: **Write Correct Word:**

1. hugged   huuged   huged   _____
2. coract   correct   coreect   _____
3. funy   funny   funnie   _____
4. happy   happie   hapy   _____
5. pupy   puppie   puppy   _____
6. comon   commun   common   _____
7. collect   colect   colecct   _____
8. bottles   botles   botlles   _____
9. diffrent different diferent   _____
10. lesson   leson   lesoon   _____
11. eror   error   errer   _____
12. pulled   puled   puuled   _____
13. begged   beged   beggd   _____
14. silli   sillie   silly   _____
15. matter   mattar   mater   _____
16. suppar   supper   suuper   _____
17. seting   setting   seeting   _____
18. jelli   jellie   jelly   _____
19. ladder   laddur   lader   _____
20. tunel   tunnal   tunnel   _____

31.4 - Rolling Objects

Name: _____

Rolling Objects
Cause and Effect Paragraph Checklist

Directions: Reread your writing carefully. Put a check in each box under Author Check as you complete each item.

Revise and Edit for the following:

1. CLARITY AND MEANING:
Ask yourself,
"Is it clear why or how this invention was created?"
"Are the three facts clear?"
"Are the facts explained clearly?"
Rewrite parts that are unclear or need revision.

AUTHOR CHECK:

2. CORRECT USE OF WORDS:
Ask yourself,
"Are specific and varied adjectives and adverbs used?"
"Is the information written in my own words?"
"Do the sentences sound good together?"
Rewrite parts that need revision.

AUTHOR CHECK:

3. CAPITALIZATION:
Use capitals at the beginning of each sentence and for proper nouns.
Make corrections if needed.

AUTHOR CHECK:

4. PUNCTUATION:
Use periods, exclamation points, and question marks.
Make sure commas and apostrophes are used correctly.
Make corrections if needed.

AUTHOR CHECK:

5. SPELLING:
Check for correct spelling.
Make corrections if needed.

AUTHOR CHECK:

Name: _____

Rolling Objects
Handwriting Practice 2

Directions:
Use the dashed lines to help you form each word. Then, write each word four more times on your own.

love

put

quick

ray

love

put

quick

ray

31.4 - Rolling Objects

Name _____

SPELLING TEST

Directions: As your teacher reads your words, write each spelling word on the blanks below.

1) _____
2) _____
3) _____
4) _____
5) _____
6) _____
7) _____
8) _____
9) _____
10) _____
11) _____
12) _____
13) _____
14) _____
15) _____
16) _____
17) _____
18) _____
19) _____
20) _____

31.5 - Rolling Objects

Name: _____

Rolling Objects
Independent Reading

Directions: Read your independent reading book for 30 minutes. When you are done, write a short summary of what you've read.

I read _____ by _____
       (book title)   (author)

for 30 minutes today.

_____   _____
    My signature   Parent/Guardian Signature

Details:

Write a short summary of what you read today:

_____
_____
_____
_____
_____
_____
_____
_____

31.5 - Rolling Objects

Name: _____

Electricity - Journal Entry

Directions: Write your response to the prompt on the lines below. Don't forget to check for complete sentences as you write.

Prompt:
What are some of the ways you use electricity every day?

Name: _____

Spelling - Electricity

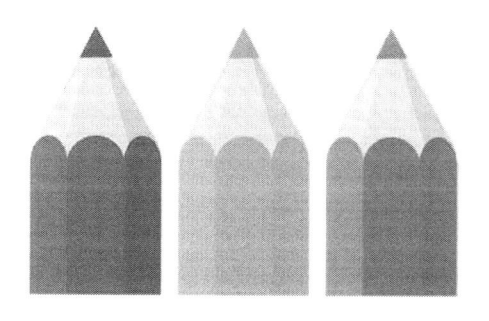

Rainbow Words

Directions:
Please choose three different colored pencils. Write each spelling word three times using each color.

pennies	_____	_____	_____
emptied	_____	_____	_____
parties	_____	_____	_____
families	_____	_____	_____
mysteries	_____	_____	_____
married	_____	_____	_____
carried	_____	_____	_____
puppies	_____	_____	_____
tried	_____	_____	_____
hurried	_____	_____	_____
ponies	_____	_____	_____
cities	_____	_____	_____
stories	_____	_____	_____
flies	_____	_____	_____

continued on the next page...

Spelling - Electricity

Rainbow Words

Directions:
Please choose three different colored pencils. Write each spelling word three times using each color.

dried _____ _____ _____

worried _____ _____ _____

cried _____ _____ _____

buried _____ _____ _____

replied _____ _____ _____

candies _____ _____ _____

Name: _____

Electricity
Descriptive Paragraph Graphic Organizer

Directions: Organize the information about your day without electricity. Think about your normal day and what would be different if you didn't have electricity. Include as many details as you can.

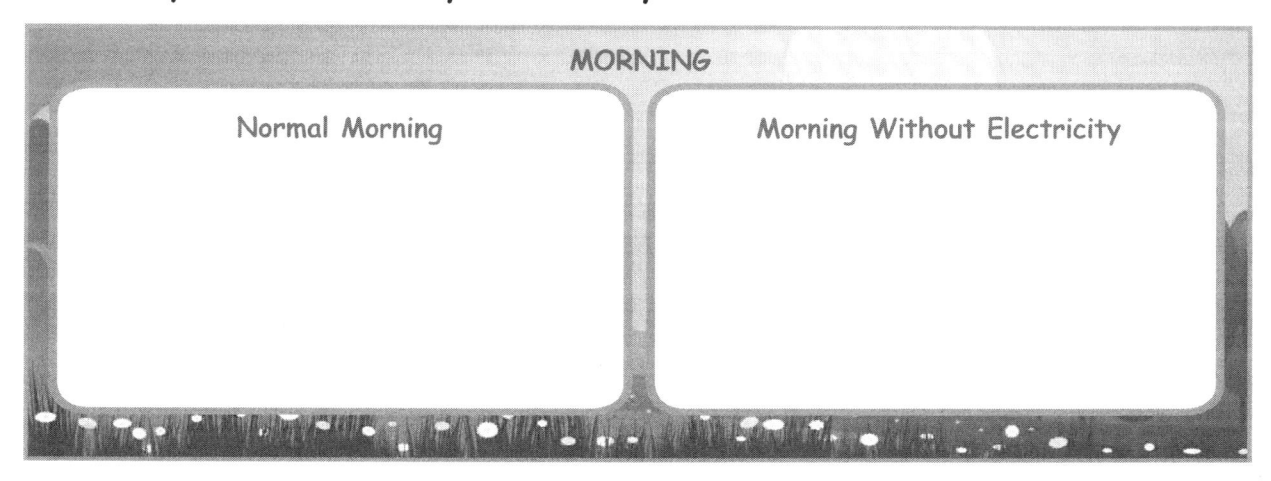

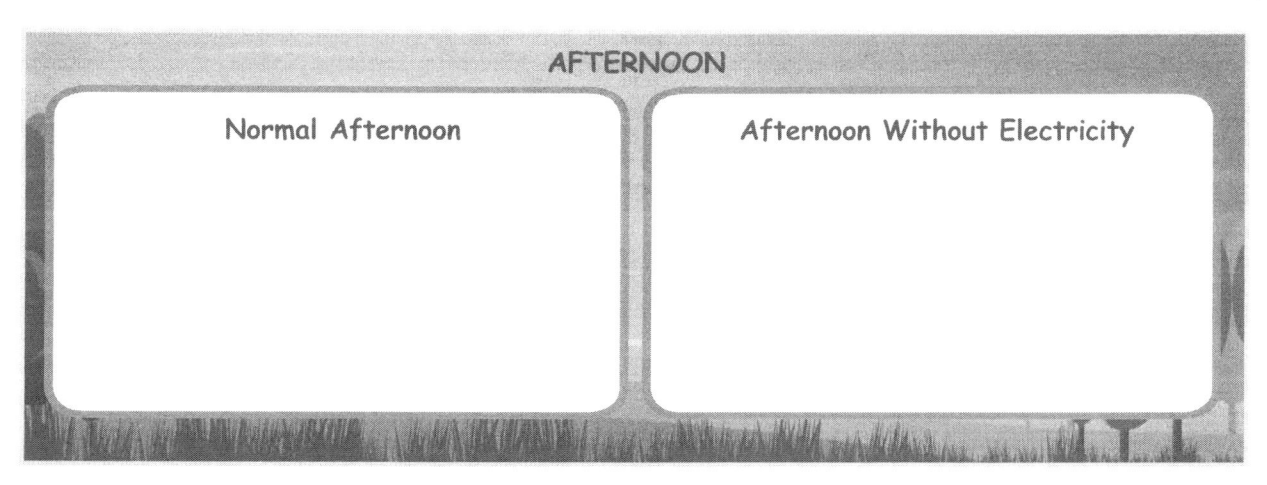

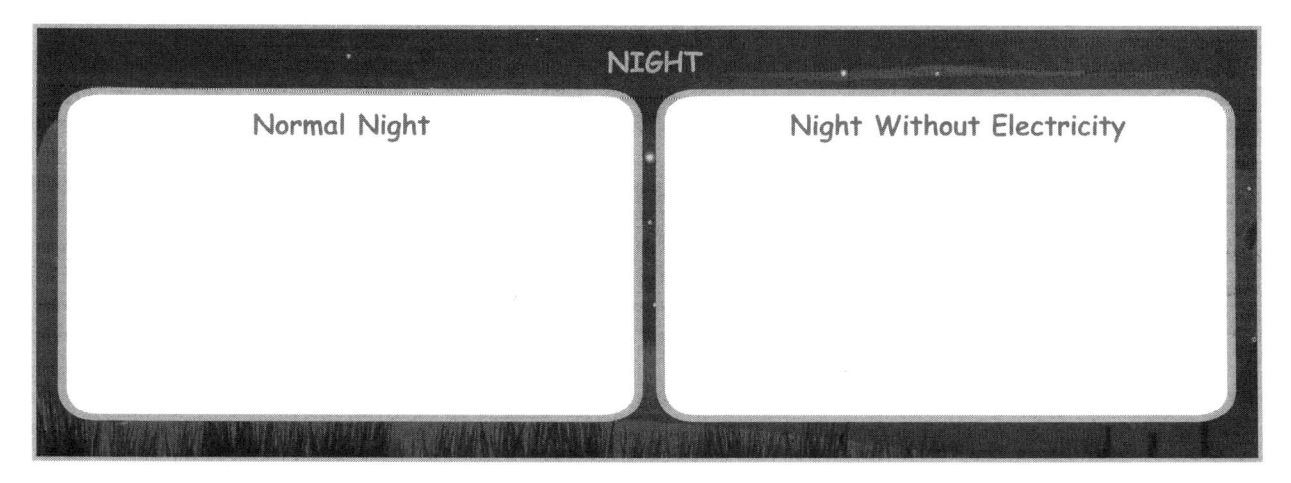

MORNING

Normal Morning	Morning Without Electricity

AFTERNOON

Normal Afternoon	Afternoon Without Electricity

NIGHT

Normal Night	Night Without Electricity

Name: _____

Electricity
Handwriting Practice 1

Directions: Use the dashed lines to help you form each word in the sentence.

The quick brown

fox jumps over the

lazy dog The quick

brown fox jumps

over the lazy dog

The quick brown

fox jumps over the

lazy dog The quick

brown fox jumps

over the lazy dog

Name: _____

Electricity
Vocabulary Crossword Puzzle

Directions:
Use the definitions to complete the crossword puzzle using your vocabulary words.

ACROSS:
3. coming after the present
4. to comprehend or understand
5. something that helps the one it belongs to

DOWN:
1. gaining or having gained wealth, respect, or fame
2. to have a strong effect on
6. a general principle or set of principles that explains facts or events of the natural world

32.3 - Electricity 156

Name: _____

Electricity
Spelling Worksheet

Directions:
Circle the correct spelling of the spelling word and then write the correct spelling of the word on the blank.

Circle Correct Spelling: **Write Correct Word:**

1. penies   pennys   pennies   _____
2. emptied   emptyed   emptyd   _____
3. partys   partees   parties   _____
4. familes   families familys   _____
5. mysteries mysterys misteries _____
6. maried   married   maryed   _____
7. caried   carried   caryed   _____
8. pupies   pupys   puppies   _____
9. tried   tride   tryd   _____
10. hurried hurryed   huried   _____
11. ponys   ponies   poneys   _____
12. citys   citties   cities   _____
13. storys   stories   storries   _____
14. flys   flies   fllys   _____
15. dried   dryed   driyd   _____
16. woried   worryed   worried   _____
17. cryed   cryd   cried   _____
18. burried buried   buryed   _____
19. replied replyed   repllied   _____
20. candies candys   candyies   _____

Name: _____

Electricity
Cause and Effect Paragraph Checklist

Directions: Reread your writing carefully. Put a check in each box under Author Check as you complete each item.

Revise and Edit for the following:	
1. CLARITY AND MEANING: Ask yourself, "Is it clear what would be different about my day without electricity?" "Are the morning, afternoon, and night all present?" "Are details explained?" Rewrite parts that are unclear or need revision.	AUTHOR CHECK:
2. CORRECT USE OF WORDS: Ask yourself, "Are specific and varied adjectives and adverbs used?" "Do the sentences sound good together?" Rewrite parts that need revision.	AUTHOR CHECK:
3. CAPITALIZATION: Use capitals at the beginning of each sentence and for proper nouns. Make corrections if needed	AUTHOR CHECK:
4. PUNCTUATION: Use periods, exclamation points, and question marks. Make sure commas and apostrophes are used correctly. Make corrections if needed.	AUTHOR CHECK:
5. SPELLING: Check for correct spelling. Make corrections if needed.	AUTHOR CHECK:

32.4 - Electricity

Name: _____

Electricity
Handwriting Practice 2

Directions:
Use the dashed lines to help you form the sentence. Then, write the sentence three more times on your own.

The quick brown

fox jumps over the

lazy dog

Name _____

SPELLING TEST

Directions: As your teacher reads your words, write each spelling word on the blanks below.

1) _____
2) _____
3) _____
4) _____
5) _____
6) _____
7) _____
8) _____
9) _____
10) _____
11) _____
12) _____

13) _____
14) _____
15) _____
16) _____
17) _____
18) _____
19) _____
20) _____

Name: _____

Electricity
Independent Reading

Directions: Read your independent reading book for 30 minutes. When you are done, write a short summary of what you've read.

I read _____ by _____
           (book title)   (author)

for 30 minutes today.

_____   _____
My signature   Parent/Guardian Signature

Details:

Write a short summary of what you read today:

_____
_____
_____
_____
_____
_____
_____

Name: _____

Attraction - Journal Entry

Directions: Write your response to the prompt on the lines below. Don't forget to check for complete sentences as you write.

Prompt: Write an adventure about Captain Magnetism. Explain how he saved the day using his magnetic power.

_____
_____
_____
_____
_____
_____
_____
_____
_____
_____
_____
_____
_____
_____
_____
_____

33.1 - Attraction

Name: _____

Spelling - Attraction

Rainbow Words

Directions:
Please choose three different colored pencils. Write each spelling word three times using each color.

careless _____ _____ _____

sleepless _____ _____ _____

clueless _____ _____ _____

harmless _____ _____ _____

bottomless _____ _____ _____

wireless _____ _____ _____

spotless _____ _____ _____

worthless _____ _____ _____

helpful _____ _____ _____

cheerful _____ _____ _____

painful _____ _____ _____

careful _____ _____ _____

graceful _____ _____ _____

harmful _____ _____ _____

continued on the next page...

Spelling - Attraction

Rainbow Words

Directions:
Please choose three different colored pencils. Write each spelling word three times using each color.

playful _____ _____ _____

useful _____ _____ _____

colorful _____ _____ _____

joyful _____ _____ _____

thankful _____ _____ _____

stressful _____ _____ _____

Name: _____

Attraction
Narrative Graphic Organizer

Directions:
Fill the boxes below with information about the event you will be writing about. Include as many details as you can.

Event: _____

Beginning:

Middle:

End:

33.2 - Attraction

Name: _____

Attraction
Handwriting Practice 1

Directions:
Write your first name in cursive ten times on the lines below.
Use the letters as a guide to help you build your name.

ABCDEFGHIJKLMNOP

QRSTUVWXYZ

abcdefghijklmnopqrst

uvwxyz

33.2 - Attraction

Name: _____

Attraction
Vocabulary Crossword Puzzle

Directions: Use the definitions to complete the crossword puzzle using your vocabulary words.

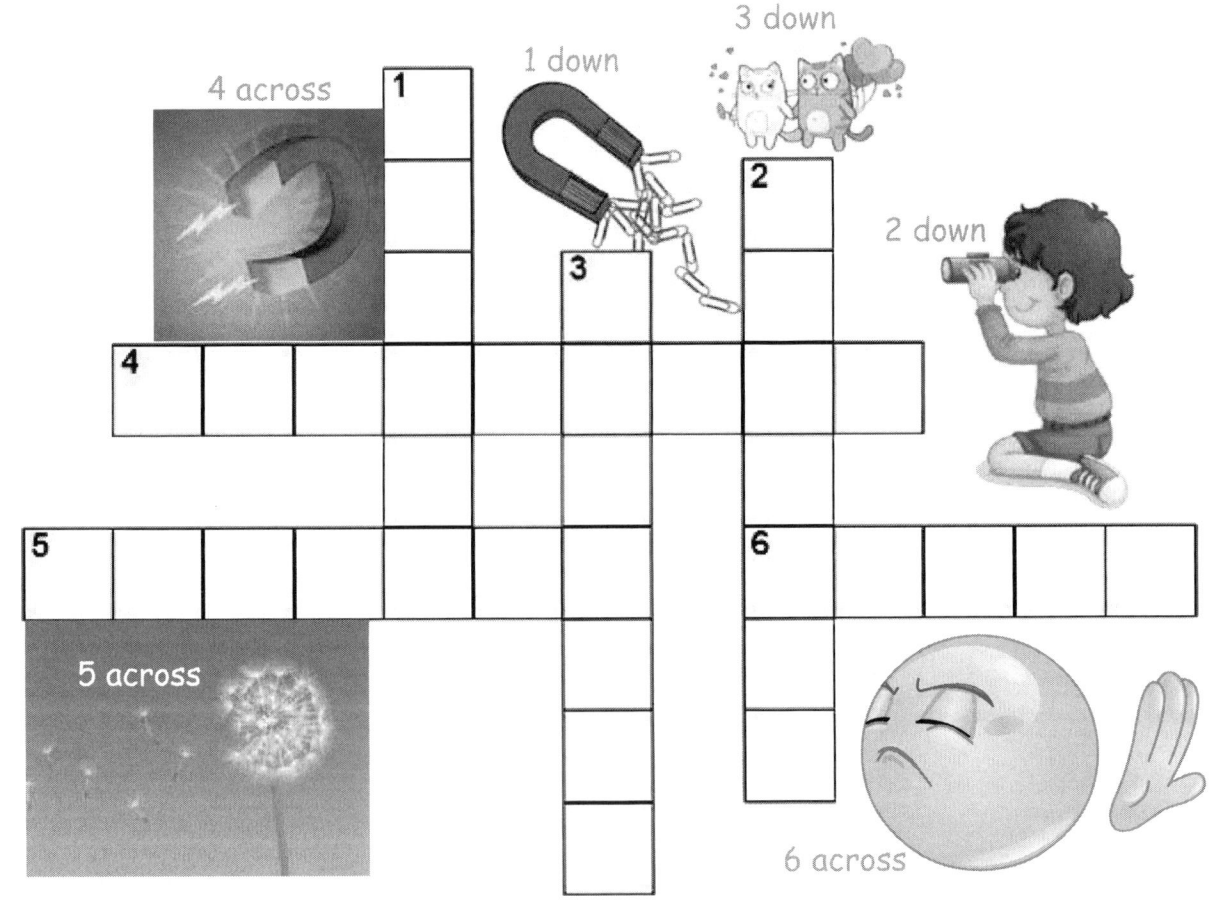

ACROSS:
4 the property of attracting certain metals or producing a magnetic field
5 to cause to separate widely
6 to push or drive back

DOWN:
1 a piece of some material that is able to attract iron
2 to watch carefully
3 to pull to or toward oneself or itself

Name: _____

Attraction
Spelling Worksheet

Directions:
Circle the correct spelling of the spelling word and then write the correct spelling of the word on the blank.

Circle Correct Spelling: Write Correct Word:

1. careless   carless   careles   _____
2. slepless   sleples   sleepless   _____
3. cluless   clueles   clueless   _____
4. harmless   harmles   harmeless   _____
5. botomless bottomless bottomles   _____
6. wireless   wirless   wireles   _____
7. spotless   spotles   spoteles   _____
8. worthles   worthless wourthless _____
9. helpful   helpfull   helpfule   _____
10. cherful   cherfull   cheerful   _____
11. painful   paneful   painfull   _____
12. carful   careful   carfull   _____
13. gracful   graceful   gracfull   _____
14. harmfull harmfule   harmful   _____
15. playfull plaefull   playful   _____
16. useful   usful   usefull   _____
17. colorfull colurful   colorful   _____
18. joyful   joyfull   joeyful   _____
19. thankfull thankful   thankeful   _____
20. stresful stressful stressfull _____

33.4 - Attraction   168

Name: _____

Attraction
Narrative Checklist

Directions: Reread your writing carefully. Put a check in each box under Author Check as you complete each item.

Revise and Edit for the following:

1. CLARITY AND MEANING:
Ask yourself,
"Is my story clear and easy to follow?"
"Can I identify the beginning, middle, and end?"
"Are details used?"
Rewrite parts that are unclear or need revision.

AUTHOR CHECK:

2. CORRECT USE OF WORDS:
Ask yourself,
"Are specific and varied adjectives and adverbs used?"
"Do the sentences sound good together?"
Rewrite parts that need revision.

AUTHOR CHECK:

3. CAPITALIZATION:
Use capitals at the beginning of each sentence and for proper nouns.
Make corrections if needed.

AUTHOR CHECK:

4. PUNCTUATION:
Use periods, exclamation points, and question marks correctly.
Make sure commas and apostrophes are used correctly.
Make corrections if needed.

AUTHOR CHECK:

5. SPELLING:
Check for correct spelling.
Make corrections if needed.

AUTHOR CHECK:

Name: _____

Attraction
Handwriting Practice 2

Directions:
Write your full name in cursive five times on the lines below.
Use the letters as a guide to help you build your name.

ABCDEFGHIJKLMNOP

QRSTUVWXYZ

abcdefghijklmnopqrst

uvwxyz

33.4 - Attraction

Name _____

SPELLING TEST

Directions: As your teacher reads your words, write each spelling word on the blanks below.

1) _____
2) _____
3) _____
4) _____
5) _____
6) _____
7) _____
8) _____
9) _____
10) _____
11) _____
12) _____
13) _____
14) _____
15) _____
16) _____
17) _____
18) _____
19) _____
20) _____

33.5 - Attraction

Name: _____

Attraction
Independent Reading

Directions: Read your independent reading book for 30 minutes. When you are done, write a short summary of what you've read.

I read _____ by _____
　　　　　(book title)　　　　　　　　　　　(author)

for 30 minutes today.

_____　　_____
　　　　　My signature　　　　　　　　　　　Parent/Guardian Signature

Details:

Write a short summary of what you read today:

_____
_____
_____
_____
_____
_____
_____
_____

33.5 - Attraction

Name: _____

Immigration - Journal Entry

Directions: Write your response to the prompt on the lines below. Don't forget to check for complete sentences as you write.

Prompt: Imagine that you had to move to another country. How would you feel? What would you expect? If you have moved to another country, write about how you felt and what you expected.

_____
_____
_____
_____
_____
_____
_____
_____
_____
_____
_____
_____
_____
_____
_____

Name: _____

Spelling - Immigration

Rainbow Words

Directions:
Please choose three different colored pencils. Write each spelling word three times using each color.

comfortable _____ _____ _____

erasable _____ _____ _____

available _____ _____ _____

portable _____ _____ _____

disposable _____ _____ _____

reusable _____ _____ _____

livable _____ _____ _____

fixable _____ _____ _____

wearable _____ _____ _____

laughable _____ _____ _____

capable _____ _____ _____

honorably _____ _____ _____

irritably _____ _____ _____

probably _____ _____ _____

continued on the next page...

34.2 - Immigration

Spelling - Immigration

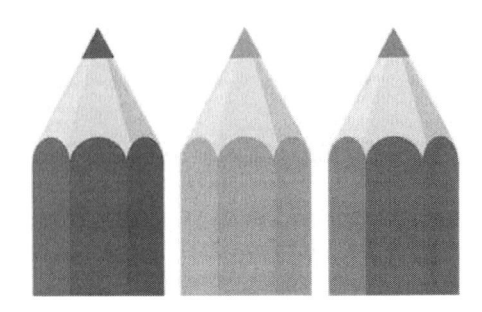

Rainbow Words

Directions:
Please choose three different colored pencils. Write each spelling word three times using each color.

miserably _____   _____   _____

noticeably _____   _____   _____

reasonably _____   _____   _____

unseasonably _____   _____   _____

Name: _____

Immigration: Biography Graphic Organizer

Directions: Fill out the sections below with information about the immigrant you will be writing about. Include as many details as you can. If you are writing about someone you know, start with some questions you would like that person to answer for you. If you are writing about a historical figure, write some questions that you will try to answer during your research online or at a library.

Immigrant: _____

Background information: Write two questions about the immigrant's background. Then find out and write down the answers to these questions.

1. _____

   _____

2. _____

   _____

Life in the country of origin: Write two things you would like to know about the country where the immigrant was born. Then find out and write down the answers to these questions.

1. _____

   _____

2. _____

   _____

continued on the next page:

34.2 - Immigration

Name: _____

Reasons for moving to the United States: Write two things you would like to know about why the immigrant moved here. Then, find out and write down the answers to these questions.

1. _____

_____

2. _____

_____

Life in the United States: Write two things you would like to know about the immigrant's life after he or she moved to this country. Then find out and write down the answers to these questions.

1. _____

_____

2. _____

_____

Name: _____

Immigration
Handwriting Practice 1

Directions: Use the letters as a guide to rewrite the paragraph below in cursive.

When I was a baby, my family came to this country from Jamaica. We love life in the United States and our Jamaican heritage as well. We still visit family in Jamaica when we can. We hope they will join us here soon!

ABCDEFGHIJKLMNOP

QRSTUVWXYZ

abcdefghijklmnopqrst

uvwxyz

34.2 - Immigration

Name: _____

Immigration
Vocabulary Crossword Puzzle

Directions:
Use the definitions to complete the crossword puzzle using your vocabulary words.

ACROSS
3   not very long, short
5   one of the great divisions of land on the globe
6   a temporary stop or rest

DOWN
1   to stick to as if glued
2   an abnormal bodily condition of a living plant or animal that interferes with functioning
4   existing in fact and not just a possibility, real

179

34.3 - Immigration

Name: _____

Immigration
Spelling Worksheet

Directions:
Circle the correct spelling of the spelling word and then write the correct spelling of the word on the blank.

Circle Correct Spelling: Write Correct Word:

1. comfortabel   comfertable   comfortable   _____
2. erasable   eraseable   erasably   _____
3. available   avaleable   availible   _____
4. portabel   portable   portabul   _____
5. disposable   disposeable   disposabel   _____
6. reusabl   reusable   reuseable   _____
7. liveable   liveabel   livable   _____
8. fixeable   fixable   fixably   _____
9. wearable   wearabel   wereable   _____
10. laughable   laghable   laugable   _____
11. capabel   capeable   capable   _____
12. honorably   honurably   onorably   _____
13. irritablie   irritably   irittably   _____
14. probabbly   probobly   probably   _____
15. miseribly   miserably   miserebly   _____
16. noticably   noticeably   noticibly   _____
17. reasonably   resonably   reasenably   _____
18. unseasonably   unsesonable   unsesunably   _____

Name: _____

Immigration
Biography Checklist

Directions: Reread your writing carefully. Put a check in each box under Author Check as you complete each item.

Revise and Edit for the following:

1. CLARITY AND MEANING:
Ask yourself:
"Is the immigrant's story clear?"
"Can I identify why this person moved to the United States and how he or she felt about it?"
"Are details used?"
Rewrite parts that are unclear or need revision.

AUTHOR CHECK:

2. CORRECT USE OF WORDS:
Ask yourself:
"Are specific and varied adjectives and adverbs used?"
"Do the sentences sound good together?"
Rewrite parts that need revision.

AUTHOR CHECK:

3. CAPITALIZATION:
Use capitals at the beginning of each sentence and for proper nouns.
Make corrections if needed.

AUTHOR CHECK:

4. PUNCTUATION:
Use periods, exclamation points, and question marks.
Make sure commas and apostrophes are used correctly.
Make corrections if needed.

AUTHOR CHECK:

5. SPELLING:
Check for correct spelling.
Make corrections if needed.

AUTHOR CHECK:

Name: _____

Immigration
Handwriting Practice 2

Directions: Use the letters as a guide to rewrite the paragraph below in cursive.

Our neighbors just moved here from Ireland. Aaron is my age, and we get along great. He was nervous about moving to the United States at first. He's glad he's here, and so am I!

ABCDEFGHIJKLMNOP
QRSTUVWXYZ
abcdefghijklmnopqrst
uvwxyz

34.4 - Immigration

Name _____

SPELLING TEST

Directions: As your teacher reads your words, write each spelling word on the blanks below.

1) _____
2) _____
3) _____
4) _____
5) _____
6) _____
7) _____
8) _____
9) _____
10) _____
11) _____
12) _____

13) _____
14) _____
15) _____
16) _____
17) _____
18) _____

34.5 - Immigration

Name: _____

Immigration
Independent Reading

Directions: Read your independent reading book for 30 minutes. When you are done, write a short summary of what you've read.

I read _____ by _____
             (book title)   (author)

for 30 minutes today.

_____   _____
      My signature   Parent/Guardian Signature

Details:

Write a short summary of what you read today:

_____
_____
_____
_____
_____
_____
_____
_____

Name: _____

Voting - Journal Entry

Directions: Write your response to the prompt on the lines below. Don't forget to check for complete sentences as you write.

Prompt: Why do you think it's important to vote?

Name: _____

Spelling - Voting

Rainbow Words

Directions:
Please choose three different colored pencils. Write each spelling word three times using each color.

know _____ _____ _____

known _____ _____ _____

knife _____ _____ _____

knock _____ _____ _____

knee _____ _____ _____

knot _____ _____ _____

knit _____ _____ _____

knight _____ _____ _____

wrong _____ _____ _____

wrinkle _____ _____ _____

wrap _____ _____ _____

wrist _____ _____ _____

wrote _____ _____ _____

wreck _____ _____ _____

continued on the next page...

35.2 - Voting

Spelling - Voting

Rainbow Words

Directions:
Please choose three different colored pencils. Write each spelling word three times using each color.

wring

write

wristwatch

gnat

sign

gnaw

Name: _____

Voting
Persuasive Paragraph Graphic Organizer

Directions: Fill out the information below with your reasons why the voting age should or should not be changed to 10 years old.

Do you think the voting age should be changed to 10 years old?

01 Reason: _____

02 Reason: _____

03 Reason: _____

Name: _____

Voting
Handwriting Practice 1

Directions: Use the letters as a guide to rewrite the paragraph below in cursive.

I went to the polls with my mom yesterday. She told me that voting is a very important responsibility and she thought very hard about who she would vote for. There were lots of people there, and we had to wait in line for a while. It was really neat to see voting in action.

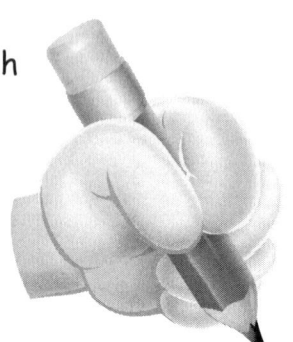

ABCDEFGHIJKLMNOP

QRSTUVWXYZ

abcdefghijklmnopqrst

uvwxyz

189

35.2 - Voting

Name: _____

Voting
Vocabulary Crossword Puzzle

Directions:
Use the definitions to complete the crossword puzzle using your vocabulary words.

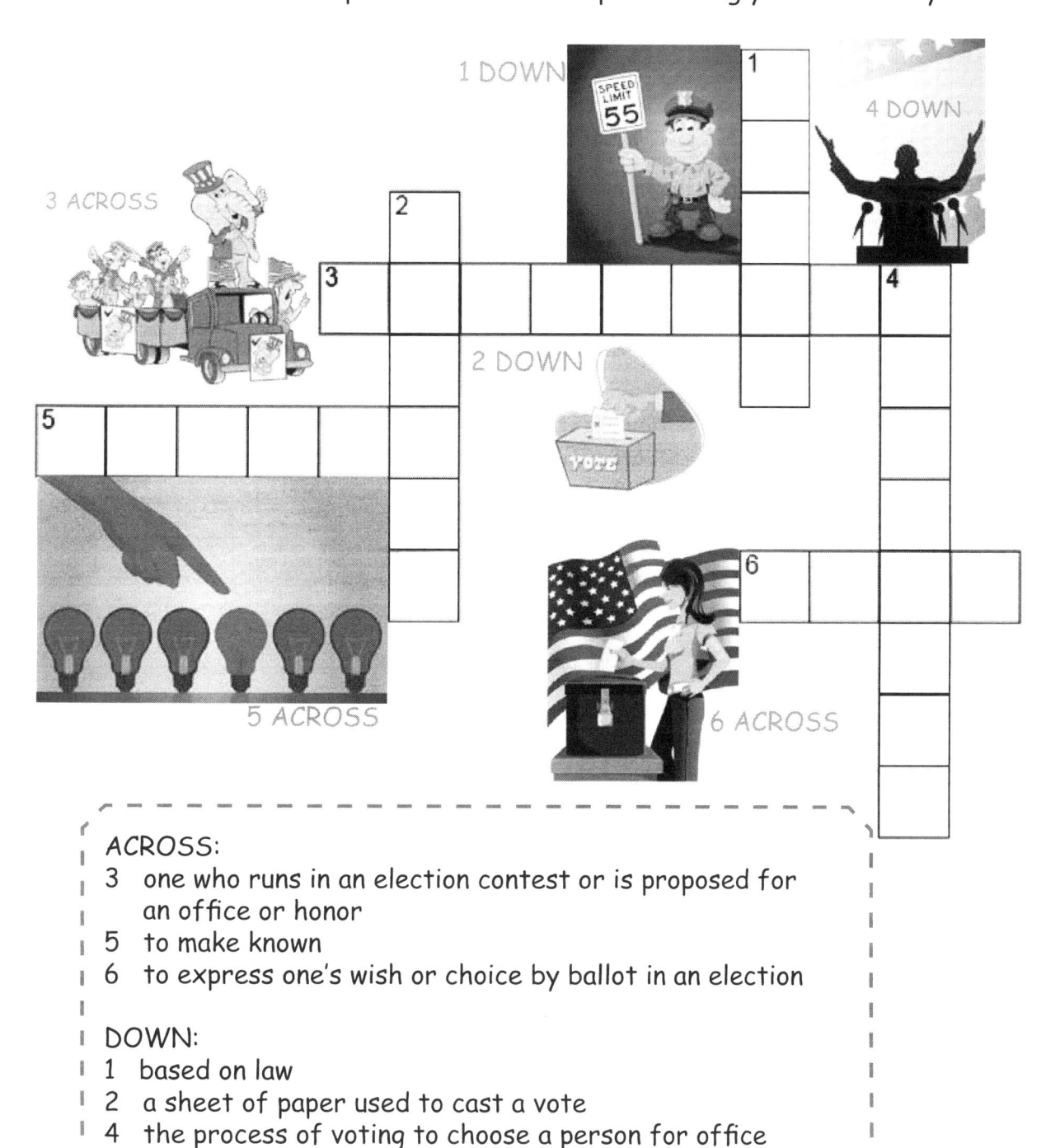

ACROSS:
3 one who runs in an election contest or is proposed for an office or honor
5 to make known
6 to express one's wish or choice by ballot in an election

DOWN:
1 based on law
2 a sheet of paper used to cast a vote
4 the process of voting to choose a person for office

35.3 - Voting

190

Name: _____

Voting
Spelling Worksheet

Directions:
Circle the correct spelling of the spelling word and then write the correct spelling of the word on the blank.

Circle Correct Spelling: Write Correct Word:

1. rist   wriste   wrist   _____
2. naw   gnaw   nawe   _____
3. knife   nife   knif   _____
4. roat   wrote   wrot   _____
5. signe   sign   siegn   _____
6. know   knoew   knowe   _____
7. wreck   reck   wrek   _____
8. gnatt   nat   gnat   _____
9. known   nown   nowne   _____
10. rinkle   wrinkel   wrinkle   _____
11. knote   knot   knott   _____
12. wronge   ronge   wrong   _____
13. kne   nee   knee   _____
14. wristwatch wristewatch ristwatche _____
15. knight   nighte   knite   _____
16. wriet   write   wriete   _____
17. knitt   nit   knit   _____
18. wring   wringe   wreng   _____
19. knok   knock   nock   _____
20. wrap   wrapp   wrap   _____

Name: _____

Voting
Persuasive Paragraph Checklist

Directions: Reread your writing carefully. Put a check in each box under Author Check as you complete each item.

Revise and Edit for the following:	
1. CLARITY AND MEANING: Ask yourself, "Is my point of view clear?" "Can I identify the three reasons why I feel this way?" "Are explanations given?" Rewrite parts that are unclear or need revision.	AUTHOR CHECK:
2. CORRECT USE OF WORDS: Ask yourself, "Are specific and varied adjectives and adverbs used?" "Do the sentences sound good together?" Rewrite parts that need revision.	AUTHOR CHECK:
3. CAPITALIZATION: Use capitals at the beginning of each sentence and for proper nouns. Make corrections if needed.	AUTHOR CHECK:
4. PUNCTUATION: Use periods, exclamation points, and question marks. Make sure commas and apostrophes are used correctly. Make corrections if needed.	AUTHOR CHECK:
5. SPELLING: Check for correct spelling. Make corrections if needed.	AUTHOR CHECK:

35.4 - Voting

Name: _____

Voting
Handwriting Practice 2

Directions: Use the letters as a guide to rewrite the paragraph below in cursive.

The new president has just been announced. Everyone's votes were tallied late into the night, but my mom let me stay up to watch. I'm looking forward to seeing what our new president will do for our country.

ABCDEFGHIJKLMNOP

QRSTUVWXYZ

abcdefghijklmnopqrst

uvwxyz

193 35.4 - Voting

Name _____

SPELLING TEST

Directions: As your teacher reads your words, write each spelling word on the blanks below.

1) _____
2) _____
3) _____
4) _____
5) _____
6) _____
7) _____
8) _____
9) _____
10) _____
11) _____
12) _____

13) _____
14) _____
15) _____
16) _____
17) _____
18) _____
19) _____
20) _____

35.5 - Voting

Name: _____

Voting
Independent Reading

Directions: Read your independent reading book for 30 minutes. When you are done, write a short summary of what you've read.

I read _____ by _____
           (book title)   (author)

for 30 minutes today.

_____   _____
My signature   Parent/Guardian Signature

Details:

Write a short summary of what you read today:

_____
_____
_____
_____
_____
_____
_____

Name: _____

Freedom - Journal Entry

Directions: Write your response to the prompt on the lines below. Don't forget to check for complete sentences as you write.

Prompt: Imagine that you are a farm animal and you have broken loose from your pen. What animal are you? What would you do with your freedom?

_____
_____
_____
_____
_____
_____
_____
_____
_____
_____
_____
_____
_____
_____

Name: _____

Spelling - Freedom

Rainbow Words

Directions:
Please choose three different colored pencils. Write each spelling word three times using each color.

speech   _____   _____   _____

child   _____   _____   _____

chance   _____   _____   _____

cheek   _____   _____   _____

chunk   _____   _____   _____

bench   _____   _____   _____

chick   _____   _____   _____

cheese   _____   _____   _____

crunching   _____   _____   _____

lunch   _____   _____   _____

teacher   _____   _____   _____

sandwich   _____   _____   _____

match   _____   _____   _____

watch   _____   _____   _____

continued on the next page...

Spelling - Freedom

Rainbow Words

Directions:
Please choose three different colored pencils. Write each spelling word three times using each color.

batch _____ _____ _____

catcher _____ _____ _____

stretch _____ _____ _____

hatch _____ _____ _____

ditch _____ _____ _____

pitch _____ _____ _____

Name: _____

Freedom
Opinion Paragraph Prewrite

Directions: Do you think that pets should have freedom? Should they get to choose where they live and live the life they want?

Opinion: _____

Reason #1: _____

Details: _____
_____
_____
_____

Reason #2: _____

Details: _____
_____
_____
_____

continued on next page:

Reason #3: _____

Details: _____
_____
_____
_____

Name: _____

Freedom
Handwriting Practice 1

Directions: Use the letters as a guide to rewrite the paragraph below in cursive.

Neat handwriting is important because we want others to be able to read our writing. Good handwriting involves properly formed letters and careful spacing. It's also important to form letters the correct height.

ABCDEFGHIJKLMNOP

QRSTUVWXYZ

abcdefghijklmnopqrst

uvwxyz

Name: _____

Freedom
Vocabulary Crossword Puzzle

Directions:
Use the definitions to complete the crossword puzzle using your vocabulary words.

3 ACROSS
1 DOWN
4 DOWN
2 DOWN
6 ACROSS
5 ACROSS

ACROSS:
3 faithful to a cause
5 an outer part or edge
6 a point beyond which a person or thing cannot go

DOWN:
1 one who shows shameful fear or timidity
2 a constant ratio between two things
4 to damage the quality or effect of

36.3 - Freedom

Name: _____

Freedom
Spelling Worksheet

Directions: Fill in the blanks with ch or tch to correctly spell each word.

1. _____ eek

2. pi _____

3. ha _____

4. di _____

5. tea _____ er

6. crun _____ ing

7. spee _____

8. _____ unk

9. sandwi _____

10. ben _____

11. stre _____

12. ca _____ er

13. _____ ick

14. ba _____

15. lun _____

16. _____ ild

17. wa _____

18. _____ eese

19. ma _____

20. _____ ance

Name: _____

Freedom
Opinion Paragraph Checklist

Directions: Reread your writing carefully. Put a check in each box under Author Check as you complete each item. Then give your paragraph and checklist to a peer for a peer check.

Revise and Edit for the following:	
1. CLARITY AND MEANING: Ask yourself, "Are details used to explain your points?" Rewrite parts that are unclear or need revision.	AUTHOR CHECK:
2. CORRECT USE OF WORDS: Ask yourself: "Are specific and varied adjectives and adverbs used?" "Do the sentences sound good together?" Rewrite parts that need revision.	AUTHOR CHECK:
3. CAPITALIZATION: Use capitals at the beginning of each sentence and for proper nouns. Make corrections if needed.	AUTHOR CHECK:
4. PUNCTUATION: Use periods, exclamation points, and question marks. Make sure commas are used correctly. Make corrections if needed.	AUTHOR CHECK:
5. SPELLING: Check for correct spelling. Make corrections if needed.	AUTHOR CHECK:

36.4 - Freedom

Name: _____

Freedom
Handwriting Practice 2

Directions: Use the letters as a guide to rewrite the paragraph below in cursive.

I love putting puzzles together. My mom and I work together to put the pieces in the right places. Sometimes we work on small puzzles, but I like the big ones. They have a lot of pieces and take a lot of time, but we are so proud of our work when we are done.

ABCDEFGHIJKLMNOP

QRSTUVWXYZ

abcdefghijklmnopqrst

uvwxyz

Name _____

SPELLING TEST

Directions: As your teacher reads your words, write each spelling word on the blanks below.

1) _____
2) _____
3) _____
4) _____
5) _____
6) _____
7) _____
8) _____
9) _____
10) _____
11) _____
12) _____
13) _____
14) _____
15) _____
16) _____
17) _____
18) _____
19) _____
20) _____

36.5 - Freedom

Name: _____

Freedom
Problem and Solution Worksheet

Directions: Identify the problem and solution from "Barb's Brilliant Plan."

Problem: _____

_____

_____

_____

_____

_____

_____

_____

Solution: _____

_____

_____

_____

_____

_____

_____

Name: _____

Freedom
Independent Reading

Directions: Read your independent reading book for 30 minutes. When you are done, write a short summary of what you've read.

I read _____ by _____
               (book title)   (author)

for 30 minutes today.

_____   _____
          My signature   Parent/Guardian Signature

Details:

Write a short summary of what you read today:

_____
_____
_____
_____
_____
_____
_____
_____